Bicycle Touring

by the editors of *Bicycling®* Magazine

 Rodale Press, Emmaus, Pennsylvania

Printed in the United States of America on recycled paper, containing a high percentage of de-inked fiber.

Senior Editor, Ray Wolf
Edited by Larry McClung
Cover photograph by Mark Lenny
Cover design by Linda Jacopetti and Karen A. Schell
Book design by Linda Jacopetti

Library of Congress Cataloging in Publication Data
Main entry under title:

Bicycle touring.

Cover title: Bicycling magazine's bicycle touring.
   1. Bicycle touring.   I. Bicycling!
II. Title: Bicycling magazine's bicycle touring.
GV1044.B53   1985   796.6   85-2226
ISBN 0-87857-547-2   paperback

2   4   6   8   10   9   7   5   3   paperback

Contents

Introduction 1

Part One: Acquiring the Right Equipment 3
How to Shop for a Touring Bike 4
Transforming Your Present Bike into a Touring
Machine 12
Racks and Panniers: Where to Put the Weight on
Your Bike 20

Part Two: Tips for Successful Touring 30
The ABCs of Training for Touring 31
Traveling Light 36
Seven Tips to Make Your Touring Easier 41
An Ingenious Repair Can Save Your Tour 45

Part Three: Planning Your Tour 50
Touring—Alone or in a Group? 51
Touring in the Winter: A Firsthand Report 57
Outsmarting the Desert Sun 63

**Part Four: Preparing and Maintaining the Touring
Body** 69
Speed Training for Tourists 70
Food for Touring 77
First Aid Kits for Tourists 84

Credits 91

Introduction

One of the great attractions of bicycle touring is the way in which it allows us to discover and express our individuality. Cycle racing, by contrast, is highly structured, imposing fairly specific and similar demands of training and technique on all participants. Bike commuting also has its structure, since it usually functions within severe constraints of time, distance, and the necessity for quick transitions between sweaty athlete and well-groomed businessperson. However, touring is only as structured as we wish to make it.

This is not to say that tourists can avoid making important decisions. On the contrary, they must choose whether to go solo or in a group, travel fast or slow, go heavily loaded with gear or light, sleep in motel rooms or under the starry sky, head north, south, east, or west. Indeed, it is precisely because cycle touring starts with few givens and opens up endless possibilities that it is such a personal experience. Touring can provide the context for forming new friendships and for strengthening the ties of existing friendships and family relationships. It can help us discover new territory or simply to encounter familiar territory in a more intimate way.

Touring by bicycle does have its constraints. It forces us to function for a period of time with a very limited set of physical possessions, to relate to the natural world with little in the way of a protective shield, to rely in particularly trying circumstances on our wits and in general on our own two legs. Because of these constraints, it can teach us important lessons about self-reliance and the joys of living simply.

Many cyclists have discovered that bicycle touring has a unique quality that enables it to serve as a method for quickly breaking through barriers that normally inhibit interaction between strangers. The tales told by cycle tourists are full of references to chance encounters that quickly blossom into warm friendships and significant, though brief, human interactions that would otherwise have never taken place. They are also full of testimonials to the fact that cycle touring offers opportunities to discover and appreciate the beauties that cannot be duplicated when traveling by any motorized mode of transportation.

This leads us to a final but important piece of advice. Tourist: beware of the speed trap! In an age when everyone seems to be looking for ways to go places and do things in as little time as possible, it is easy for us to let a hurried pattern of behavior carry over into our cycling. True, there are times when speed is useful, even desirable. We even included a chapter in this book telling you how to work on increasing your cycling speed. However, the best way to tour is to start with flexible goals, then relax and enjoy the ride, see the sights, and take the occasional detour to out-of-the-way places. So slow down and don't turn your tour into a race across the continent. Early on, decide how far you can go in a day, then plan on covering half that distance. This will help you establish a comfortable pace that will get you to your destination but leave you time to savor your experiences along the way.

The Editors,
Bicycling magazine

Part One
Acquiring the Right Equipment

How to Shop for a Touring Bike

Gone are the days when a bicycle was simply a bicycle. These days there is a bicycle made for every conceivable two-wheel pursuit. There are racing bikes and touring bikes, all-terrain bikes and commuting bikes, but even these categories are too general. Some bikes are made especially for track racing; others are built to suit the needs of competitors in criteriums, triathlons, and other types of road races. Touring cyclists, for their part, are offered a choice between bikes made for carrying light loads on day and weekend trips or longer "credit card" tours, and bikes that can handle 40 to 50 pounds of gear packed in front and rear panniers while being navigated over rough roads and mountain passes.

The truth of the matter is that, despite this specialization of function, many bikes do not fit neatly into one category. A model that some riders will consider to be a racing bike will be classed by others as "sport touring," a handy term used to refer to bikes that fit somewhere between the pure racing and touring models. Moreover, since most cyclists cannot afford to maintain a whole stable of highly specialized bikes, they manage to find multiple uses for whatever bikes they possess. Though we don't recommend it, there are people who have set out across the country on racing bikes. Others, more rationally, have tried and discovered that all-terrain bikes with fat, knobby tires, work quite well for taking extended tours of places like Maine and Vermont.

Thus, when it comes to selecting a bike for touring, a lot

4

of factors have to be taken into account. First, you have to decide whether you want to buy and equip one bike specifically for touring, while maintaining an additional vehicle or two for other purposes. If that's the case, you then must decide what type of touring you want to do. If, for example, you intend to pack no more than 15 or 20 pounds of gear and travel over fairly decent roads, a short-wheelbase sport touring bike with narrow clincher rims will suffice—provided you pick your way around potholes, crawl over railroad tracks, and are comfortable with slightly squirrelly handling. On the other hand, if you plan to haul 40 to 50 pounds of gear over rough roads and Rocky Mountain passes, you would be wise to choose a bike designed to handle such weight and terrain.

Recognizing that different tourists have different needs and tastes in bikes and the fact that some daring souls will make do with vehicles not designed for the tasks to which they are put, we cannot say specifically which bike you should buy. All we can do is provide you with some general guidelines and information on the subject, pointing out differences between "sport tourers" and "loaded tourers." The rest is up to you, your own good judgment, and perhaps a bit of trial and error.

Photograph 1–1. The Specialized Sequoia is a touring bike suitable for all-around general use.

Sport Touring Bikes

Sport tourers are the jack-of-all-trades of the bicycling world. If you're willing to accept some compromises, a single sport tourer can take the place of a whole stable of racing, touring, and recreational bikes. With more responsiveness than long-wheelbase, loaded tourers and a more comfortable, stable ride than all-out racing bikes, sport tourers have captured the lion's share of the derailleur-equipped bicycle market in this country.

Faced with stiff competition for the recreational dollar, and bolstered by a favorable exchange rate when purchasing foreign-made components, manufacturers have responded by offering upgraded equipment and improved frames on their "meat-and-potatoes" lines of sport touring bikes. Aluminum wheels; chrome-molybdenum steel tubing; lighter, better-working alloy components; and attractive finishes were available on bikes in the under $300 price range at the time *Bicycling* magazine conducted its summer and fall, 1984, road tests.

Five mass-produced sport touring models were included in these tests. They were the Centurion LeMans RS, SainTropez 440, Ross Signature 290 S, Motobecane Super Mirage, and Panasonic Sport 1000. These bikes, representative of the dozens of similar designs available at the time, ranged in price from $180 to $299. Off the shelf, all these bikes would be at home on weekend club rides, quick jaunts around town, and daily commutes to school or work. Their predictable, easy handling make riding them a breeze even for inexperienced cyclists. When people say they own "a 10-speed," 99 out of 100 times they are talking about a bike like one of these.

The most expensive sport touring bike in this test group, the Centurion LeMans RS, could easily qualify as an entry-level road racing bike. All the test riders were impressed by its quick, sure cornering and its confident, road-holding descent, not to mention its striking good looks. Change the freewheel to one geared for racing and you would have a comfortable racing bike. Add a set of good racing wheels and you would really be in business. Yet, equipped with the components selected by the manufacturer, the Centurion LeMans is quite acceptable for light touring. This is a good example of the versatility of good sport touring bicycles.

Photograph 1–2. The Centurion LeMans is a good example of a sport touring bike that could easily be adapted for use in road racing.

Loaded Touring Bikes

For an extended trip, where you'll be spending long hours in the saddle, day after day, comfort and easy riding are the prime concerns. A true touring bike will thus have a frame designed to provide a smooth and stable ride while carrying heavy loads over rough roads. Ideally, such a frame will have a longer wheelbase and shallower head angle than racing bikes. It will be equipped with wide-profile tires and a broad range of gears, including those provided by a "granny ring"—the small, third chainwheel on the crankset, needed to pilot a loaded bike up a steep hill. Steering on these bikes is sure and easy so the rider can take in the surroundings instead of just concentrating on riding a straight line.

The longer 17½- to 18½-inch chainstays found on loaded tourers do more than increase rider comfort. By moving the rear wheel farther back, they allow the rear panniers to clear the rider's heels and still nestle their load ahead of the rear axle.

Positioned farther back, the heavy panniers might allow the tail to wag the dog, a problem when trying to safely negotiate a corner.

On a racing bike, light weight is achieved with a compromise in strength, and stiffness is maintained with steep angles and short tubes. A loaded touring bike requires a strong frame to resist deflections caused by the heavy loads positioned at its extreme ends. That particular type of stiffness is usually achieved with heavier tubing since the stays must be longer for pannier clearance. The soft, touring ride is retrieved with laid-back angles and lots of fork rake, not light tubing, so don't look to save any weight in the frame of a true touring bike.

Making Sense of Frame Dimensions

When you look at a set of specifications on a particular bicycle, you find a lot of numbers that you may not fully understand, so here are the key frame dimensions and what they tell you. Illustration 1–1 will help you visualize the discussion.

Photograph 1–3. The Raleigh Kodiak comes equipped with wide, knobbed tires and steers easily even when heavily loaded.

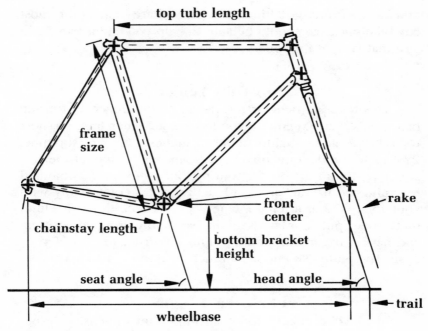

Illustration 1–1. Basic frame dimensions.

Frame Size

The number given for the size of a frame should be equivalent to the length of the seat tube. The problem is that different manufacturers measure seat tube length in different ways. Some measure center-to-center, i.e., from the center of the bottom bracket to the center of the lug joining the seat tube and the top tube. Others measure all the way to the top of the seat tube. The most common sizes available range from 19 to 25 inches.

What you need is a frame size that fits your leg length, but you must also figure in the optimum seat height for the type of riding you will be doing. Touring cyclists generally pick a larger frame and set the seat lower than racers because this makes the handlebars higher and allows them to sit upright, but you don't want a frame so tall that you cannot comfortably straddle the top tube when standing flat-footed on the ground.

The point of all this is that reading numbers in a list is not the best way to select a frame. You really need to see the bike, straddle it, climb in the saddle, and take it out for a spin. Once you have a pretty good idea of what you are looking for, most any bike salesman should be able to help you find a frame of a size that is right for you.

Top Tube Length

This tends to be short on racing bikes, longer on touring bikes. However, exceptions abound. For a 23-inch frame, a short top tube would be slightly under 22 inches; a medium top tube, 22¼ inches; and a long top tube, 22¾ inches. No top tube length is inherently unsuitable for touring, but you want a combined top tube and handlebar stem length that fits comfortably with your torso and arm length. One way to check the fit is climb on the bike, put your hands on the bars in the dropped position, and have a friend suspend a plumb line from the tip of your nose. The plumb should fall an inch behind the handlebars.

Chainstay Length

Now we're talking about an important dimension, especially if you are planning to carry panniers. Longer stays allow more of your pannier weight to be located between the axles, improving weight distribution. They also make the frame more shock-absorbing. A good old-fashioned touring frame will have chainstays approximately 18 inches in length, whereas the stays on an all-out racing frame will measure between 16 and 16½ inches. Many sport touring bikes, including the best in our test group, have sub-17-inch stays, making them more suitable for fast recreational riding than for serious touring. For heavy-duty touring, you would be wise to look for a frame with chainstays over 17 inches.

Bottom Bracket Height

A high bottom bracket is very valuable on a criterium bike because it allows you to pedal through corners. But on bikes used for road racing and touring, bottom bracket height is not a terribly important dimension. Still, bikes designed for loaded touring generally have relatively low bottom brackets for a lower center of gravity. The lower your weight sits between the wheel axles, the more stable your bike will be.

Seat Tube Angle

Seat tube angles usually vary from 72 to 75 degrees, with an occasional 76-degree angle found on a very small frame. Seat tube angle is used in combination with saddle adjustment to locate the cyclist in proper position over the pedals. It's not particularly touring-related, although some people will tell you it is. Any problems that you may have with your bike's seat angle can usually be solved by adjusting your saddle forward or backward.

Head Tube Angle

This is another key dimension on a touring bike. Angles of head tubes on the sport touring bikes in our recent test group ranged between 72 and 74 degrees. Those on the loaded tourers were essentially the same, ranging from 72.5 to 74.5 degrees. Actually, a slacker angle (70 to 72 degrees) makes a bike absorb road shock better. However, you probably won't find a touring bike with a head angle slacker than 72 degrees, unless you choose to tour on an all-terrain bike. Three of the ATBs in our recent test group had angles of 68 degrees, while the fourth had an angle of 70 degrees.

Fork Rake

This is keyed to head tube angle. The fork rake will be chosen to give the correct amount of steering stability with a given head angle. Some people will tell you that more rake makes a bike more stable, but this is not necessarily so. Less rake makes a bike more stable at high speeds, such as on downhill descents. But at the lower speeds characteristic of long-distance touring, and with the added weight of loaded panniers, extra rake is needed for stability. Moreover, on any bike, there is a direct correlation between rake and head angle. The shallower the head angle, the more rake is needed.

Wheelbase

This dimension is essentially determined by all the preceding ones. A rule of thumb is that for a medium-size (23-inch) frame, a wheelbase of 40 inches or less is good for racing; 40 to 41 inches is about right for a sport touring model; and 41 to 42 inches is suitable for a loaded tourer. This is pretty much what we found on the bikes in our test group. But note that smaller frame sizes have shorter top tubes, so the overall length of bikes smaller than 23 inches will be a bit less. And even on ordinary frame sizes, top tubes may vary by more than an inch. Thus, a frame with front and rear end geometry designed for touring can have a short top tube and will end up with a wheelbase of only 40 inches. Such a bike may still be quite suitable for touring.

Buy New or Upgrade?

Now that you have some understanding of how to make sense of manufacturers' specifications, you are ready to visit your local bike shops and select the perfect touring machine. But wait! Before you cough up $500 for your dream machine, maybe you should take a long, hard look at the trusty bike parked in your garage. Perhaps it can fill the bill for your touring needs, at least until you find out just how serious a bicycle tourist you really are.

Transforming Your Present Bike into a Touring Machine

The reappearance of the loaded touring bicycle is a curious thing. In the early '70s, this type had a brief run in American shops. Usually of French origin, it arrived in a near-complete state of touring readiness, with racks, fenders, lights, and a wide-range 15-speed gearset mounted on a frame of moderate angles, long wheelbase, and straight-gauge tubing. The only concession to American taste, as compared to the home-market European version, was the fitting of 27 × 1¼-inch tires and wheels in place of fatter tires. Put panniers on one of these tourers, and it was ready to go. With a price tag comfortably less than $150, these 30-pound bikes should have sold like hotcakes.

They didn't. Americans preferred their bikes stripped, without the clutter of fenders, lights, and racks. However useful, these made the bike weigh more, and everybody knew extra weight made you slower than Eddy Merckx's grandmother. So American bike shops began selling lightweight bikes that were stripped of all but the bare essentials. And when customers wanted to go touring, they went back to the dealers and bought touring gear: racks, wide-range gearsets, and sometimes even fenders and lights. "Aftermarket," the dealers call this trade. Unfortunately, for the customer it is much more expensive to buy a stripped bike and add accessories to it, than it is to buy the bike with the gear already attached by the bicycle factory.

Reverse Synergy

This is not to mention the struggle that must be undertaken by the consumer to fit these accessories to a stripped bike. Anyone who has done it knows that bikes possess reverse synergy; adding stuff interferes with the works of the whole. Install a rear rack, and the dropout mounting screw snatches at the chain. The fender stays don't want to fit around the luggage rack, and when you do get the fender on, the rear wheel doesn't want to go back in. No clearance. Rats! Pack the bike with luggage, and the rear reflector is covered, so you're less visible to the motorist who might run you down at nightfall. Rats again!

Eventually, you get things sorted out, but you wish the factories would do all the fitting. Not only could they do it cheaper, they could do it better. When factories do it, everything fits as if it were made to, which, of course, it is. But don't blame dealers and bike makers for this uneconomic and exasperating situation. They supply bikes and accessories as Americans prefer to buy them. However, signs indicate that preferences are changing.

At the beginning of this decade, Miyata, noting an increasing tourist trade, tentatively introduced a made-for-touring model. It had no fenders or lights but came with racks, a heavy-duty 40-spoke rear wheel, and a wide-range 15-speed gearset, all mounted on a frame designed to absorb road shock and give a comfortable ride. An additional nice touch was supplied by cantilever brakes, which are superior stoppers.

The initial production of the Miyata Model 1000 was limited, just enough to test the market. The Japanese company was not eager to get burned. However, ten years and a boom in touring made a difference for the Japanese. Model 1000s sold out in weeks. Since then, many other manufacturers have joined the tour bike bandwagon, as can be seen from the frequency with which touring bikes have been reviewed in *Bicycling* magazine's road test articles in recent years.

For the well-heeled aficionado, of course, tour bikes have never been absent. Custom frame builders, both in the United States and in Europe, have always cheerfully made the very finest in top-line tourers. What has changed is that now you can go down to your nearest well-stocked bike shop and buy a high-quality touring bike right off the rack.

Introduction of the new tourers presents both an opportunity and problem for prospective tourists. The opportunity

Photograph 1—4. First-rate custom touring bikes like this have always been available from custom frame builders. Now they can be found in any well-stocked bike shop.

occurs to the first-time bike buyer who is afforded a choice not previously available. Choosing a good tourer is as simple as selecting a model equipped with factory-applied touring gear. They are more expensive than the French offerings of 15 years ago, but then their equipment is fancier, too. And of course, inflation has had its impact on prices. These tour bikes will serve well for day trips and around-town use, too. The racks can be taken off for this type of riding, if you so choose.

If the new bikes are designed and advertised for touring, does this mean your old, reliable 10-speed is incapable of filling that role? Not necessarily. Some bikes are more suitable for touring than others, but nearly any sort of bike of decent quality can convey itself, its rider, and the rider's gear on the open road with aplomb.

Selection of a touring cycle is a very personal thing, depending a lot on the style in which you wish to travel. If you're a credit card tourist—you carry bare minimum clothing, and your main touring gear consists of credit cards to pay for everything—a super racer may be your ultimate tourer. For most of us, however, bicycle touring means travel with bike as beast of roughly 40 pounds of burden.

Hallmarks of a Touring Bike

Bear in mind that while almost any good bike can become a tour bike, some bikes are more adaptable to touring than others. A longer wheelbase is helpful. That means 40 inches plus rather than 40 inches minus (an inch is a long way in frame design). Longer wheelbase usually allows for more clearance at tires, permitting fender mounting and easier wheel removal. Racing bikes, by contrast, may have tight clearances and lack eyelets on dropouts. Eyelets are needed for securing racks and fenders.

Your bike doesn't have eyelets? Don't give up on it. Your dealer can supply adaptors to secure racks. Usually the presence of eyelets and a longer wheelbase are indicators that the frame designer has incorporated slightly less steep frame angles and complementary steering geometry. The former inclines frame tubes to absorb a bit more road shock. That's appreciated when you're on the bike for several days. The latter makes for more stability when carrying touring equipment.

The weakest link in most touring systems is the gearing. The typical sport touring bike, for example, has a gear range of approximately 40 to 100 inches. This can be seen in Table 1–1, which shows the gear set-up on a popular sport touring bike profiled in *Bicycling* magazine's 1985 Buyer's Guide. In case you are unfamiliar with the method of calculating gear inches, the formula is as follows: A (the number of front chainwheel teeth) divided by B (the number of rear cog teeth), then multiplied by C (the diameter of the rear wheel), equals gear inches. Thus, a bike with a 42–52 chainwheel combination, a 14–16–18–21–24–28 freewheel, and 27-inch tires has a gearing system that ranges from 40 to 100 inches as shown in the table.

Bikes designed for loaded touring typically come equipped with a triple chainwheel, greatly expanding their range of gearing. Thus, for example, the Bridgestone T700, has a gear range of 22 to 96 inches, thanks to a 28–44–50 crankset and a 14–17–21–26–34 freewheel. Though this was the set-up that offered the lowest gears among the five loaded tourers tested for the '85 Buyer's Guide, even it might not suffice in all situations. Our most macho hill climber, who normally sneers at weaklings who add "granny" rings to their cranksets, had second thoughts during these tests. Halfway up a mile-long hill on a bike loaded with 50 pounds of soybeans, he began running out

	No. of teeth on chainwheels	
	42	52
14	81	100
16	70	87
18	63	78
21	54	66
24	47	58
28	40	50

No. of teeth on rear cogs

Gear inches

Table 1–1. Gearing Chart

Photograph 1–5. One of the most valuable things you can do to transform your reliable 10-speed into a touring bike is to equip it with a suitably small third chainring for navigating those steep hills.

of spin in the 30-tooth chainring and 30-tooth rear cog combination that provided the lowest gear on the bike. At that point, he began wishing for a 24- or 26-tooth granny ring. When it comes to loaded tourers, the lowness of the low gear is more critical than the wideness of the overall gear range.

   Some people tour on tubular (sew-up) racing tires but not as many as in the past. It's too expensive. While the trend in clincher (conventional) tires has been to emulate the skinny silhouette of tubulars, "less is better" does not apply to touring tires. More is better. Skinny tires and rims may look fast and sporty, but they lack shock-absorbing capacity beneath a touring load. Standard-size 27 × 1¼-inch or 700C × 32-mm rubber keeps bumps a little farther from the rims.

   Here's further advice on tires: start a tour on new ones. For some reason, new tires are more resistant to puncture than those that have known pavement for a while, even if tread thickness is comparable.

On a touring bike as on any rim-brake bike, rims should be aluminum. Why? When wet, aluminum rims brake yards better than chromed steel rims, and they give a much nicer ride. Also, if you're touring England or a similar clime where you can count on rain, mount fenders, and be sure the front fender has the flexible flap at its lower end to keep the splash off your shoes.

Speaking about Spokes

When picking out a touring bike, cyclists often pay little attention to spokes, but do consider them, most especially the rear ones. These have been given a bum deal by bike designers. When bikes were 1-speeds, rear wheels were symmetrical, and spokes had a better time of it. But when designers invented derailleur gears—and we love them for that—they packed five sprockets on the rear hub, where there had been one sprocket. To make room, the right hub flange was shoved over. Hence nonsymmetrical ("dished") rear wheels were created. Out of this arrangement, the right-side spokes—those next to the free-wheel sprockets—came off with a disproportionate share of the rear wheel load.

Most of your 40-pound load of gear goes over the rear wheel, and it is "dead" weight; it doesn't stand on the pedals going over bumps like you do. So a bump gives a loaded bike a brutal jolt to the rear wheel, and because of asymmetry, the greatest part of the jolt is delivered to the right-side spokes. Thus, it's usually the right-side spokes that break, the ones most difficult to replace because of the freewheel.

How do you prevent spoke breakage? By taking several precautionary steps. First, as we have already suggested, you should fit your bike with wide, cushy tires. You should also use heavy-duty spokes on your touring wheels—the thicker 14-gauge variety in place of the usual 15-gauge or double-butted types. Then—and this may be more important than spoke size—make sure they are tight.

There is still a theory going around that long-lived touring wheels possess slightly twangy spokes so as to provide a degree of "give" upon bump impact. Writing in *American Wheelmen* for August 1980, John Forester, an engineer and former League of American Wheelmen president, described some simple wheel load tests he conducted that disproved this theory. Tightly spoked wheels, Forester concluded, subject individual spokes to less stressful cyclical loading than do loosely spoked wheels. The greater the weight carried, the more advantage accrues to the tightly spoked wheel.

If your rear wheel is like most rear wheels that have seen use, it may be a bit gamey. The rim may have flat spots and be somewhat out of round. The spokes may look frozen to the nipples, as some of them probably are. Seeing the condition of your wheels, you may look at the rest of your bike and find other parts that are tired and neglected.

In Praise of a Trusted Two-Wheeled Friend

What you need on tour is not so much a new bike as a well-prepared bike—a reliable bike that will be trouble-free far from home and help. It could be a mistake to assume that a new bike will be more reliable than Old Trustworthy. Remember, your old bike is broken in. The several bearings have long since bedded down and been adjusted. The wheels, also broken in, were tightened by your dealer when you took the bike in for its free 30-day checkup—likewise the cables and derailleurs. And if anything was amiss as a result of a factory assembly mistake, it has long since been put right.

This is not so for a new bike. Take a shiny new machine right off the rack—even one of the built-for-the-task tourers, pack it and hit the road, and there is a chance that sometime later down the road your new bike will let you down. Maybe a bottom bracket cup will back out, ruining the axle. Maybe a crankarm will work loose on the squared axle end, damaging an expensive crankset. And it's almost a certainty that if your tour is very long, there will be broken right-side rear spokes.

None of this will be the bike's fault, either. Whether new or old, tour bikes need preparation if they are to be reliable. Before you set out on your old bike, it needs to be overhauled and equipped for the journey. If you elect to buy a new bike, it must be broken in and given a post-break-in tune-up.

Among tourists, there are those who prepare with the me-

ticulousness of astronauts. They lube, check, and adjust everything, from pedals to brake blocks, and replace suspect parts.
Then there are those who carry out what little preparation time
affords in a last-minute flurry. Here's a bit of advice for the latter
folks.

If Old Trustworthy is to be your mount, take off its rear
wheel and proceed to the local friendly bike shop. Buy new
tires. Ask to have the wheel examined and, if necessary, attended
to. A good mechanic can tighten and true a wheel in minutes.
Don't take the entire bike into the shop, because at the height
of the touring season the mechanic has a month's backlog of
repair work. Take just the wheel in, and he'll probably do the
job on the spot.

If you must buy a new bike, explain to your prospective
supplier your near-imminent departure. Select your bike and
agree to buy if the dealer agrees to perform the all-important
tune-up promptly when you bring the bike back after you've
ridden it hard for a couple of days. If the dealer can't work that
into his schedule, try elsewhere until you find a dealer who can.

Locating a cooperative dealer shouldn't be difficult. Dealers
are as fascinated with the adventure of bike touring as are most
people you'll meet. Many will go out of their way to be helpful,
which is one of the nice things about touring.

Racks and Panniers: Where to Put the Weight on Your Bike

You would think that by now all the basic stuff of bicycle
engineering had been sorted out. After all, people have been
making bicycles for well over 100 years, and bicycles are so
simple. You can merely look at one and figure out how it works.
At least, that's what you would think.

That's what Jim Blackburn thought, too. Blackburn is the

California industrial designer who, in 1975, looked at an imported bike rack about to be marketed by a friend. "I can make a better one than that," Blackburn told his friend. Blackburn, fresh from collecting a second college degree, anticipated a career as a design consultant. Today Jim Blackburn is America's—and perhaps the world's—leading source of quality, lightweight racks.

Each year the Blackburn firm churns out hundreds of thousands of bicycle racks, bottle carriers, and associated touring items. This manufacture is carried out not far from the garage where Blackburn's first bicycle rack was assembled on the now-familiar pattern of bent and welded aluminum rods. Since that first garage-built rack, the Blackburn rear carrier has remained basically the same—although with numerous subtle changes, resulting in a gradually improved product.

The process of evolutionary improvement is one that Blackburn views as compatible with the history of bicycle design itself. The history is an example, Blackburn says, of what designers call "vernacular design." Although bicycle historians labor to establish which individuals—ranging back to Leonardo and beyond—made which particular contributions to bicycle development, from an industrial designer's point of view, the bicycle wasn't designed so much as it evolved inevitably. And while it has undergone considerable refinement, the basic "safety bicycle" (as it was once called) has remained unassailed for a century.

An appreciation of this history makes a designer of bicycle products respectful of tradition. When better products are made, they will usually be further developments of traditional ones. Usually. Following this line of thinking nearly led Blackburn to stick his foot into a very awkward bucket. It also led his firm into a modest research project, the conclusions of which will interest touring bicyclists and any others who need to carry goods on their bikes.

Blackburn's Embarrassing Discovery

The route to these conclusions was inadvertent. In 1980, Blackburn, having got his manufacturing operations humming after a move into new, larger quarters, resumed the search for product improvements. His attention turned to the lower-position front and rear panniers seen on some touring bikes in France and in photos of bikes the Japanese supply for the Asian touring market.

Here was a way of carrying gear on a bike that ought to offer significant advantages over the conventional American handlebar bag and rear pannier rig. Low panniers lower the center of gravity. That has a good effect on any vehicle. But accepted though they were by the French and Japanese, low-position panniers had somehow escaped introduction to Americans. Blackburn resolved not to neglect this marketing opportunity further.

Front and rear "low-rider" pannier rack designs were worked up. It wasn't easy. Providing sufficient rigidity was a problem, especially with the rear rack. In order to clear a rider's pedaling feet, low-mounted rear panniers had to be located farther back, almost entirely behind the rear axle. That meant the rack structure had to be cantilevered rather far behind most of the bicycle frame.

But it is the designer's work to solve such difficulties, and so sure was Blackburn that the new racks would work well— as they seemed to in around-the-block spins—that production planning proceeded while a few prototypes were made up for final field testing. One prototype set of front and rear low-riders was lent to Terry Shaw, owner of Shaw's Lightweight Cycles, a local shop.

Shaw, about to embark on a tour of the Northwest coast, replaced his conventional Blackburn racks with the prototypes the night before boarding a flight to Portland. After his first ride with the new racks at the Portland airport, he wished he hadn't.

"As soon as I got on the bike, there were incredible stability problems," Shaw says. "It would develop a shimmy at low speeds. I had to go across the Longview Bridge, which is narrow, loaded with trucks, and windy, on a weaving, unstable bike. That was an experience, I'll tell you."

As the tour progressed, Shaw experimented with repacking. Gradually he shifted weight to the front panniers. By trip's end he was loading about 90 percent of his gear into the front bags. This produced a stability as impressive as the initial instability.

Back in San Jose, Shaw told Blackburn he was onto a good thing with the front rack, but that the rear was terrible. Blackburn was skeptical. What about the Japanese and French? Shaw produced his bike, packed it, and sent Blackburn off on a ride. Convinced, Blackburn put the entire low-rider project on hold.

Back to the Drawing Board

Blackburn then sat down with his design assistant, Jim Gentes, to figure out what had gone wrong. They decided that a failure of basic design analysis had occurred. They knew how to make good racks. What they didn't know enough about was where cargo ought to be carried on a bicycle.

So Gentes was assigned to research the question. First he searched the literature. He read the standard texts and studied articles in scholarly, technical magazines like *American Physics* and *Journal of Applied Mechanics*. Gentes discovered what other students of bicycle design have before him: that the way bicycles—and motorcycles—steer and handle defies easy mathematical analysis. In this respect, bicycles are like boomerangs. People know how to make them, but scientists have a hell of a time trying to explain what makes them work.

Recently, Gentes learned, some attempts have been made to develop mathematics to describe more exactly the factors affecting motorcycle stability and handling. The results are formidable, being what engineers dryly refer to as "rather complicated equations."

Almost no mention in the literature was made of what Gentes was concerned with, the placement of weight, but it did offer models to emulate. When mathematical theory failed, scientists resorted to experiment. Via methodical trial-and-error, they rode and observed bicycles, and even if they didn't understand exactly why things happened, they reported as best they could on how they happened.

So Gentes and Blackburn elected to experiment. They would try every practical placement of weight on a normal touring bike and find out what worked best. Their test rig, built by Gentes, consisted of Blackburn's 23-inch touring bicycle fitted with sheets of plywood on either side of both wheels, plus racks

as necessary. Touring packs could be shifted quickly to any
location on the plywood, like workshop tools on a pegboard.
Panniers, rear packs, and handlebar bags were gathered. Mounting them in various configurations, Gentes took a series of test
runs through a short, low-speed slalom course, recording his
times and his impressions of bike behavior.

As a test rider and performance analyst, Gentes was ideally
suited. Like Blackburn, he is a graduate of the San Jose State
industrial design program. He is also a former national junior
cyclo-cross champion, and he has competed in Europe. "I know
how a good bike is supposed to handle," he says.

Photograph 1–6. Centering part of the weight of your touring gear
on your front wheel can actually make your bike more stable.

To exaggerate handling effects, the test bags were deliberately overloaded. Panniers carried 20 pounds of sand each. Handlebar bags, when used, carried 25 pounds, adding to a total of 80 pounds on most test runs. Ordinarily, Blackburn cautions, tourists should reduce their luggage rate to no more than 40 pounds. In the less stable test configurations, the overloading provoked serious and sometimes unmanageable handling deficiencies.

The tests confirmed Shaw's conclusions about low rear-mounted panniers located behind the rear axle; weight carried there was unwieldy. But tests also indicated problems with a popular touring accessory: the large handlebar bag. Actually, handlebar bags comprise half the sales of some American touring accessory manufacturers. They are convenient repositories for things tourists want ready at hand, and they are a means to "get weight up front."

Moving weight forward seems a good idea. If all the weight of touring gear is placed at the rear in conventional panniers and atop the rack, the center of gravity of the entire load resides slightly behind the rear wheel center. This geometry produces a levering action that, on a heavily loaded bike, almost lifts the front wheel when the rider isn't aboard. Restoring balance by transferring some of the load to the front wheel would have obvious benefits.

Test Results

However, moving weight forward is not a good idea when the load goes into a handlebar bag, Gentes found. "This was one of the worst configurations," he says. Conventionally mounted front panniers were much better, he reports, and low-mounted front panniers were better still.

After the slalom tests, Gentes made higher-speed runs on steep, winding Shannon Road in Los Gatos. Some of the least stable setups, including those using a large handlebar bag, were eliminated from the high-speed test series, as Gentes was a willing test rider but not a fool-hardy one. Even so, some of the runs down Shannon were tight-lipped, brakes-on-all-the-way affairs.

The high-speed test series was considered important, since one of the papers on motorcycle analysis had indicated that significantly different forces may affect handling at high speeds. In some cases, a machine with innocuous low-speed characteristics may provide a disaster at increased velocity.

After the test, Blackburn and Gentes assembled their findings into a succinct, illustrated article. This they published, not in a technical journal, but in a brochure, where it is more accessible to bicyclists. Some bicycle dealers may still have copies. If not, you can request one direct from Jim Blackburn Touring Performance Products, 75 Cristich Lane, Campbell, CA 95008.

There are some general statements about bicycle handling and the sources of bicycle stability found in this brochure with which we would quibble. But technical quibbles aside, the tests and conclusions of Blackburn and Gentes concerning the best ways of arranging a load on a bike are a genuine and highly useful contribution to basic knowledge about bicycling.

The Weight Distribution Tests

After trying various combinations of weight distribution on their test bike, Blackburn and Gentes settled on four combinations that best illustrate their test results. These are shown in the four illustrations that follow. In the first example, a set of large rear panniers is fastened to a rack so that most of the weight is above and behind the rear axle. No front panniers are used. Instead, a large, heavy handlebar bag is mounted on the front of the bike. This combination is probably the most common one used by touring cyclists, but Blackburn and Gentes found that it created so much front wheel shimmy that they could only ride slowly and were not able to take the bike through the downhill test.

The second combination distributes weight equally between front and rear panniers, all mounted high, above the axles. A small handlebar bag was also carried on the bike. This system, which has attained some popularity, worked much better than the first. Though, with 40 pounds of weight up front, the test bike tended to oversteer.

The third system involves a small handlebar bag and panniers mounted low on both front and rear. Placing weight low in front was not too difficult, but because of the need for heel

Illustration 1–2. A combination of large rear panniers and large handlebar bag.

clearance, the rear bags had to be placed behind the rear axle axis, which caused a whipping action when the bike was ridden. Also, the carrier, being structurally larger, had to be heavier but could not be rigid. Each rotation of the crankarms created an oscillation in the carrier, which was difficult for the rider to compensate for. Overall, Blackburn and Gentes found that the low-front/low-rear combination does not handle well. They don't recommend it.

Illustration 1–3. Equal weight in front and rear panniers, along with a small handlebar bag. All panniers are mounted high.

Illustration 1–4. A small handlebar bag is used along with low-mounted front and rear panniers.

The final set-up illustrated involves mounting medium-size panniers above the rear axle as far forward as possible on the rear carrier and centering medium-size front panniers on the front wheel. Once again, the handlebar bag is kept small. Blackburn and Gentes found this system to give by far the best handling with heavy weight. No frame whip was noted, downhill runs were safe, and steering felt secure. A bicycle loaded in this

Illustration 1–5. A small handlebar bag is combined with front and rear panniers. The front panniers are centered on the wheel; the rear are mounted in the standard position above the axle.

way will certainly respond slower than one with no weight but may in fact be more stable.

Blackburn and Gentes found through their extensive tests that, while evenly distributing weight between front and rear panniers works well even when all are mounted high, lowering the weight in front improves a bike's handling. And, whereas loaded front panniers can enhance the stability of a bike, a loaded handlebar bag has the opposite effect. It destabilizes steering. Therefore, handlebar bags, handy as they are for carrying maps, cameras, and food, should be kept small.

So when you set out to shop for racks and panniers, find a combination that will distribute the load on your bike in the best possible way. Sometimes compromises must be made, as for example when cantilever brakes interfere with the forward placement of rear panniers. But, with patience and careful attention to the match between machine and equipment, you can transform your bike into a safe and comfortable touring vehicle.

Part Two
Tips for Successful Touring

The ABCs of Training for Touring

Training for any sport or strenuous activity is to some extent an individual matter. Even the experts do not always agree on the best technique. And when it comes to training for bicycle touring, consider the following observation by John Rakowski, a veteran cycle-tourist who has ridden not only around the perimeter of the continental United States of America but around the world. In *Adventure Cycling in Europe* (Emmaus, Pa.: Rodale Press, 1981), Rakowski writes:

"An active, recreational bicyclist can hone himself into a keener physical condition through daily rides and commuting. Once on a tour, though, the conditions change. At home, he rests between 50-mile rides taken on weekends, and he eats and sleeps in a comfortable home. On the road, he'll be riding those distances for days at a time—with the added burden of a 40-pound load—and he'll have to do without the familiar comforts. That routine will tell after a while. No amount of artificial training situations will get a person as ready for the long haul as will a part of the trip itself."

The longer the tour you are planning, the truer Rakowski's words may be for you. The reminder to ease into an extended trip is a good one, especially if you are cycling across a continent or around the world! As the tour progresses, you will gradually adjust to the regimen. Midway through, you will probably feel stronger than when you started.

Ironically, a short tour may require you to start out in better shape than a long tour because the pace will probably be more brisk, and you don't want to spend most of the trip feeling uncomfortable. Of course, there are exceptions. *Bicycling* magazine's managing editor, Susan Weaver, recalls that her first bicycle tour was a lazy 100-miler broken evenly into four days. She meandered through flat Louisiana bayou country, indulging in small-town café meals and stopping often to tour historic plantation houses. And since the mileage was modest, she was able to do it on no more training than her regular five-mile (one-way) bike commute.

But if you are seriously considering doing some bicycle touring, chances are you intend to travel farther and faster than this and will encounter some hills and head winds along your route. Some preparation is advisable. Moreover, Rakowski's comment about the inadequacy of "artificial training situations" was not aimed at the raw recruit but at the "active recreational bicyclist" who is already accustomed to 50-mile weekend rides.

Photograph 2–1. Participation in regular group rides is one good way to build a foundation of physical conditioning before setting out on a tour.

Cyclists of this type already have a good foundation for coping with the rigors of touring.

At the outset, you should forget those stories you've heard about undaunted types who, with no cycling training at all, hop on their loaded 10-speeds and ride across the country. The fitter (or luckier) ones manage by keeping their mileage under 50 miles a day at first and gradually adapting to the stress. But for every one of them there is a wilted soul who packs it in and takes the bus home or, on a tour accompanied by a motor vehicle, spends much of the day riding in the "sag wagon."

So be wise and prepare yourself. Whether your goal is to develop endurance for day rides, weekend tours, or extended trips, the basics of sensible training are as easy as ABC. And there is no need to approach the process grimly; fitness training can be fun.

Aerobic Conditioning

The key to developing endurance is through aerobic exercise. On a bike, the idea is to ride at a steady pace (no coasting) and to raise your heart rate high enough to create a training effect but not so high that you wear yourself out too quickly. How fast is that? After a while, you will be able to tell simply by how you feel; you should break a sweat but still be able to talk. In the meantime, there is a scientific way to judge how hard you are working, a formula based on heart rate devised by Dr. M. J. Karvonen.

First you must compute your maximum heart rate. For a man, this is age subtracted from 220; for a woman, age from 226. Then, determine your resting heart rate by taking a one-minute count while still in bed, just after waking in the morning. Subtract the resting rate from the maximum and multiply by 0.6. Add to this your resting rate, and you'll have the minimum rate you want to hold while riding. This is a conservative figure, and many people will want to train harder. To find the upper limits for your training pulse, multiply the difference between your resting and maximum rates by 0.8 (superfit athletes may push their pulse rate into the 0.85 range) then add your resting rate. The range between these two pulse rates gives you quite

a bit of leeway for establishing a training pace that feels pro-
ductive for you.

Taking an exercise pulse on your bike is a little tricky. But
when you're comfortable riding one-handed, you can take a
pulse at your neck while coasting briefly during a workout. Press
your neck lightly, just enough to feel the pulsations and be sure
to use your fingers, not your thumb, as it has a pulse of its own.
Take the pulse for six seconds, then multiply by ten to get your
rate per minute.

Begin Gradually

Just what this means in terms of miles and pace will vary
with each person. If you are already riding regularly and want
to increase your training effort, a good rule of thumb is to add
to your weekly mileage by no more than 8 to 10 percent. If
you're really new to cycling, begin with rides every other day
at first or three times a week. If commuting is feasible, it's a
good way to get some bike miles in on a regular basis. After a
week or so, you should feel ready to take at least a short ride
five or six days a week. Allowing yourself one rest day per week
is a good idea.

A widely accepted rule for everyone who rides almost daily
is to alternate hard workout days with easy days. Monday and
Friday would be good easy days since you will probably ride
long on the weekends. As you begin to develop endurance,
progressively longer back-to-back rides on Saturday and Sunday
are important; include hills if you expect them on your tour. If
you want to do a moderately long ride during the week, Tuesday,
Wednesday, or Thursday would be good.

Take some of your training rides with the full load you plan
to carry on the trip. This should help you become used to the
way your bike handles with a load. It may also convince you
that some of those "essentials" aren't so essential after all!

Cadence

Any resemblance between a slow, old-fashioned meat grinder
and your legs going around on the pedals should be eliminated

as quickly as possible. A good, lively pedaling rhythm is your ticket to raising your heart rate and achieving the desired training effect. It is also the most efficient way to ride. If you have never counted cadence, it is easily done by counting the number of times per minute one of your feet goes full circle on the pedal. Strive for a pedaling cadence of 70 to 80 rpm at least; with training, you may learn to favor 80 to 90, as many experienced riders do. These figures, of course, are for flat ground; your cadence will slow on the hills if you run out of low gears to shift into.

A cadence this fast may not feel natural when you first try it. As a matter of fact, it may feel pretty bad, and you'll have a hard time keeping your upper body still as you churn your legs. But in time, you'll learn to pedal smoothly and swiftly, without rocking your hips in the saddle, and the benefits will be worth the trouble of learning. You'll go faster without wearing out your legs pushing those big gears.

Maintaining your cadence should guide you in gear selection. Choose a gear that lets you spin without feeling that you are struggling to make the pedals go around. Aside from the fun of coasting down a hill, if you feel the need to coast to let your legs rest when you're riding the flats, you probably need to gear down.

The basics of cycling training are really as simple as this. Just be sure to allow yourself plenty of time to reach the endurance level you need before setting out on your tour. If you begin your training with little previous aerobic conditioning, allow yourself several months to get in shape. Those of you already accustomed to an active schedule of cycling, running, and/or other aerobic activities, may find you need much less preparation time. Be sensitive to your body and develop the training schedule that is suited to your needs. But above all, be patient and don't neglect to enjoy the process. Touring may be your goal, but training can have its pleasures too.

Traveling Light

When Reinhold Messner scaled Mount Everest in the summer of 1980, it was a climb noted more for what the effort lacked than what it accomplished. The climb was a radical new approach to mountaineering—going light and fast, "alpine style." There were no hordes of porters to carry hundreds of pounds of equipment in a slow-moving process of establishing base camps. Strike fast and quick was the novel philosophy followed by Messner's party.

As distant as mountaineering seems to be from cycling, the "lighter is better" philosophy of travel was destined to filter its way down through the various levels of outdoor endeavors—backpacking and cross-country skiing, among others—to the two-wheeled community. After all, cyclists have always prized lightness when it comes to equipment.

The impulse to "go light" involves more than just equipment, however. It includes the notion that a certain freedom is generated when traveling light, allowing greater distances to be covered and making a fuller appreciation of the eventual destination possible. If you have ever labored at five mph up a long, steep grade, your bike fully loaded with touring gear, you may have wondered if there was a better way.

While touring on a bicycle is supposed to be the ultimate in freedom of travel, it is possible to become a prisoner of your equipment. If you want to travel light, it is possible to get by for a week or more on the road with only one large bag, a pair of water bottles in cages, and a well-pocketed cycling jersey. This is the method of travel adopted by Robert Templin, co-holder of the trans-continental tandem record, set in 1979, on a ride from Santa Monica, California, to New York City.

Hotels, Hostels, and Hospitality

Obviously, some adjustments are necessary when you decide to eliminate your sleeping bag, tent, and other camping gear that once burdened your touring bike. You are able to travel faster but must plan your trip much more carefully. Unlike

Photograph 2–2. Staying in a motel or hostel frees you from the necessity of carrying camping gear along on your tour. Just remember to make reservations well in advance.

camping, where there is some flexibility in the day's destination, going light necessitates the use of prearranged accommodations—a friend's home, motels, or hostels among other possibilities. Economy motels can be found in most parts of the country, but reservations are usually needed in advance.

If your bike tour is your only vacation for the year, you might want to splurge and go first-class. One possibility is to join the Bed and Breakfast League, Ltd. (2855 29th St., N.W., Washington, DC 20008). Borrowing from European tradition, the League is an organization of host members—mostly in the United States—who rent you a room for the night in their homes and serve a continental breakfast. Reservations can be made in advance, and major credit cards are usually accepted. Accommodations start at around $20 for a single room.

Several national and international organizations (for example, Touring Cyclists' Hospitality Directory and the L.A.W.'s Hospitality Home listing) cater to the more thrifty "exchange traveler"; members of the organizations open their homes to each other. It's a great way to make new friends and learn more about the area you're touring through. (Here are the pertinent addresses: Touring Cyclists' Directory, c/o John Mosley, 13623

Sylvan, Van Nuys, CA 91401 and Membership Directory/Hospitality Home List, League of American Wheelmen, P. O. Box 988, Baltimore, MD 21203.)

Now, of course, if you are endowed with an outgoing personality, you may want to try the approach of some cyclists we know who have found accommodations quite often by meeting people along the way and getting invitations home with them. Of all the possibilities mentioned, as you probably guessed, this approach is the least dependable course of action.

Through a process of trial and error (mostly error he says), Rob Templin found a system of equipment and clothing that works well for light travel. (Like all such undertakings, you'll need to find what works best for you.) Templin uses a large handlebar pack, with 600-plus cubic inch capacity, mounted on a frame for stability, to handle all the gear he needs when going on trips of up to two weeks duration. He recommends the selection of a handlebar pack with at least one large main compartment and several smaller ones to facilitate easier organization of your belongings.

Since large handlebar bags create stability problems for many bikes, you may prefer to purchase a bag that can be mounted under the seat, or you can use a pair of small front panniers instead. Just remember not to load the panniers to the brim.

Double Duty

Just as important as what you carry your gear in is the gear itself. The first and most important rule of going light is to make each piece of equipment, where possible, serve double duty. For instance, Rob Templin carries a pair of lightweight running shoes that he uses for off-the-bike activities. In a pinch, they can also serve as cycling shoes if your regular ones self-destruct. Templin also prefers the extremely compact racing "flat" to the bulkier "touring shoes" because the racing shoes are easier to pack. Some riders save space by selecting "touring shoes" that can be worn both on and off the bike, eliminating the need for alternate footwear.

A Gore-Tex windbreaker or shell garment is another necessary item for the "going light" traveler. Clothing made with

Gore-Tex, a breathable but waterproof laminate, is very versatile foul-weather gear, which is also excellent at shutting out chilly early morning air. Stay away from the heavier model jackets, though; these are not only quite expensive, they are also too heavy and bulky for most needs. Combine a lightweight Gore-Tex shell with a wool cycling sweater, and most of your upper body clothing needs will be taken care of. As an extra bonus, these jackets are great for around-the-town use or other outdoor activities. A lightweight polypropylene T-shirt (most outdoor shops carry these) will allow you to get the most out of your wool jersey by wicking away body perspiration to the outer surface. Cotton and wool fabrics absorb water; polypropylene clothing does not.

For the lower extremities, a pair of wool tights and cycling shorts complete the traveling outfit. The tights can also serve as around-the-motel or home attire, if you get a style like the Santini "warm-ups," which have a stitched-in crease, tight zippered cuffs, and matching jacket. Templin says he has had no problem wearing the tights and a Gore-Tex shell to restaurants or for sightseeing at the end of a cycling day. It might not be the most fashionable clothing around, but it will more than suffice. A pair of ultra-light nylon running shorts and a regular T-shirt can serve as lounging wear inside your motel room.

For both touring and racing, Templin prefers to wear cy-

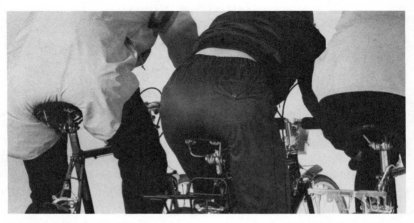

Photograph 2–3. Lightweight, waterproof clothing combined with regular wool cycling tights make good traveling outfits.

cling shorts that have a cotton-knit material in place of the usual chamois. This material makes the shorts easier to wash and quicker to dry. If you cannot locate this type of shorts in a store or catalog, you can have someone replace the liner on a regular pair.

Cameras and Books

Other small amenities that Templin takes along on tours include a full-frame 35-mm camera that is about the size of a pack of cigarettes (excuse the comparison); a pair of wool arm warmers that turn a short-sleeve jersey into a long-sleeve one; two spare sew-ups under the seat (or a folded clincher, depending on which wheels are being used); a few spare tools (spoke wrench, cluster remover, Allen wrenches, small screwdriver, etc.); patch kit and glue (with sew-ups); a spare T-shirt; and, occasionally, a paperback book. You'll probably need to modify your "must take" list somewhat to include small but important items like sunscreen and sunglasses. In warm-weather riding, all your clothing should just fit into your handlebar pack (or small panniers) and the pockets of your jersey. If it doesn't, something has got to go.

On-Tour Scenario

How does the "going light" system work? A typical day might be something like this one, which was part of a week-long tour taken by Rob Templin down the Pacific coast from San Francisco to San Diego several summers ago. Even though it was summer, the early morning ocean air was chilly, so full warm-ups were worn for the first few miles of the day. As the day warmed up, the outer wool garments were taken off and stored in the front handlebag's main compartment for easy access. The only hitch in this "stage" of the day was a slow leak in the rear tire 40 miles into the ride. Part of the evening's "recreation" would be fixing the flat.

Templin and his traveling partner arrived at the motel (reserved weeks before) early in the afternoon after having completed the scheduled 90 miles in a respectable, even if tailwind-aided, time. It did not take them long to get cleaned up, change into running shorts, tights, and T-shirt and wash clothing for reuse the following day.

Laundry facilities were close by on this occasion, but often the pair have had to use a sink and regular hand soap to clean shorts and jerseys. Drying has been accomplished using everything from a room heater to a light bulb. But be careful when trying unorthodox drying methods since polypropylene has a tendency to melt under extreme heat. Templin found that out the hard way when a light bulb melted part of his shirt on one trip. Wool clothing can be just as tricky when placed in a commercial dryer.

During the racing season, "going light" is the way Rob Templin gets in miles in different locales; he finds it an entertaining way to train. In the off-season, it's the way he chooses to travel and relax while maintaining a suitable level of fitness.

Perhaps this style of traveling does not appeal to you very much; "going light" is certainly not for everyone. But for a cyclist who never uses his or her bike when going on a camping vacation, it might prove to be a viable option. And those of you who are in the habit of touring with a full load of gear may, on occasion, find this alternative style of travel a refreshing diversion from the regimen of regular touring.

Seven Tips to Make Your Touring Easier

Bicycle touring is a highly individual sport. Every experienced tourist you meet will have plenty of stories to tell and lots of advice to offer about how you should prepare yourself and your bike and what you should carry with you on your tour. Of course, no two tourists or tours are precisely alike, and no one has the final word on what you individually should do. But, the more ideas you have available, the better prepared you will be to make good choices. In that spirit, we offer the highly personal observations of a veteran cycle-tourist by the name of Harvey T. Lyon.

A Few Things Learned the Hard Way

Through my years of touring, I've come to one conclusion: the most important thing to pack in your panniers is common sense. A little good judgment will ensure as pleasant and painless a trip as possible. Here are a few pointers I've picked up along the way.

Water

If you are riding in fairly high heat, then you can't drink too much water too often. I mean it: drink water until your eyeballs are floating. Otherwise, if you are alone, with no one else to pace you, by late afternoon you will be dehydrated. A simple test proves your need for water: you can drink five or six quarts of water on a long day's ride and never need to urinate.

Plastic

I'm blushing on this one. In past years I did a little show in a laundromat, when I would finally reach one. Under my clothes I had on a bathing suit. I'd walk into the laundromat, kick off my shoes, take off my socks, shirts, pants and throw them, along with everything else, into the machine. This year after three weeks on the road, I didn't need to. The reason: plastic. I had everything packed in separate plastic bags, some for clean, some for dirty. The result, for instance, was that the wash-and-wear suit that I carried was in fine shape. After three weeks the jacket, which I had worn much less than the pants, didn't even need washing. On-the-bike clothes went in one pannier, off-the-bike clothes in the other.

There's another reason for keeping your clothes—and your other gear—in plastic bags. Simply stated, panniers aren't waterproof. In your first downpour, you'll discover that panniers get clammy, and maybe even wet inside. Your clothes, your first aid kit, and your food . . . all will get wet.

Many cyclists prefer stuff sacks to plastic bags. They ⸌ elegant (and more expensive). Among plastic bags, the favorites are Zip-Locs. Extra-heavy-duty Zip-Locs are sold in camping supply stores.

Dips and Surges

One of the hardest things for me to learn is that my energy does not run on at a steady pace. There have been times (I confess) when I've actually gotten off the bike to see if something was stopping the wheels from turning more easily. (There wasn't.) Don't fight those shifts. Go with them.

I remember times when a slight rise had me huffing and puffing in a very low gear—and 30 minutes later, I was climbing steadily up switchback roads on a mountainside. Gear up on the surges, down on the depths. Don't get dismayed in the dips—they pass; and don't overextend yourself on the surges—they pass, too.

Rest

Which brings me to a point on which some riders will disagree: if you are riding a long distance on your own, take regular rest intervals, maybe 10 minutes every hour or 20 out of every 90 minutes, or whatever. Don't skip them because you feel fine or are worried about getting someplace. However, if you are wearing down at day's end, don't rest so frequently that you lose your pace and rhythm.

Touring and Touristing

You have a different feeling for countryside you have ridden through than that which you idly watch through the window of an air-conditioned tour bus, and that is only the beginning of the difference, especially if you are solo touring. But, here or abroad, touring is a great way to see the country and its people, and a poor way to see the sights.

My usual practice in a large city is to spend the first day riding the city at random, getting lost time after time, missing what I miss, seeing what I see. I plan now to add as standard operating procedure a half-day or even full-day city tour on a sight-seeing bus. In cities like Athens that are dull for touring but great for touristing and which are confusing as well, such a trip orients you for future riding and forestalls friends with questions. "Did you go to x? Did you see y?" Don't be dissuaded because common to all the sights and often blotting them out is the presence of other tour buses and neck craners. Take them for what they are worth.

Tires, Tubes, and Helmets

A few years ago, in April, I rode to New England. My local bike expert urged me to use thorn-resistant tubes. I was reluctant: they are enormously heavy and the weight is in exactly the wrong place, and they are also very hard to change. But I did it and also put on a new front tire. I didn't ride all the way to New England (snow in the Midwest), but I did ride around 600 miles on that trip.

I don't know what my subsequent mileage has been (it includes a Bucharest-Athens trip), but that tube is still in there—not a flat. So is the tire.

I stand six feet three inches and weigh about 210; those tubes have served me well except that getting spin is considerably harder because of the weight. Not to have a single flat in over three weeks of touring including bricks, gravel, and cobblestone is more than just luck.

Everyone has moments of extreme klutziness on a bike. I am no exception. While paying attention to everything but the wet patch on a downhill street in Athens, I swerved inappropriately and fell down pretty hard. But because I was wearing my Bell helmet, my only injuries were bruises. (And Greek shopkeepers came running to the rescue, providing me with wonderful care.)

That's the nice thing about wearing a helmet. You can fall over without doing in your skull. It beats the alternative—and I know: in my pre-helmet days I once woke up in the emergency room of a Polish hospital!

Saddle Height

This is the most embarrassing of all, and I have saved it for last. On a trip to New Hampshire, I pulled both Achilles tendons and rode on them for several days. The wonderful family that I stayed with in Bennington sent me over to an orthopedic surgeon. Since he was also a cyclist, he didn't bother to tell me that I shouldn't ride. He just gave me lots of good advice on how not to damage the tendons anymore.

He came out and looked at my bicycle and told me to lower the saddle. I had the saddle set as I thought proper, so that I had just about full extension at the bottom of the stroke. He told me to drop it until there was a definite bend in the knee. I did so. I made it across Vermont and New Hampshire, and I wound up without permanent injury. I have since kept my saddle down a half to an inch lower than I used to keep it and have not had any further trouble with my tendons. When I mentioned this to my partner, Lee Katz, he looked at me as if any sensible person would have known this all the time, and showed me the various pictures of racing riders around his store. In none of these could you see a fully extended or almost fully extended position.

So much for confessions. Enjoy your touring.

An Ingenious Repair Can Save Your Tour

The tourist's nightmare: a breakdown in the hinterland with no repair parts. And when some parts fail, you don't have to be in the hinterland to have a problem. For Ron Reed, it was his crankset. Leaving Chicago with no tools, he compounded that mistake by riding on after the bolt retaining the left arm of his Shimano Selecta crankset loosened. Within the hour, the aluminum crankarm was spinning on the spindle, and Ron was reduced to coasting and pushing. But his breakdown occurred in the outskirts of Springfield, Missouri, a city of over 100,000, so he hoped to find a quick replacement.

David Weems and Mike Murphy happened to be in the city that day and overheard Ron explaining his problem to a couple of cyclists near a bike shop. Having built many bicycles from junk parts, David and Mike suggested trying to repair the crank. The cyclists laughed, but Mike went to his pickup and got an Allen wrench that fit the crank bolt.

With the crank removed, the damage was obvious. The ridges that normally fit the grooves in the spindle were chewed off flush with the valleys. (The Selecta crankset uses a splined connection instead of a square taper.) David and Mike took the crank into the bike shop. The man behind the counter said, "parts for a Selecta?" and laughed. He mentioned two other shops in town, then laughed again. The good news from those places was that they could fix Ron's bike—after a new crank arrived. The bad news was that it would take ten days at one shop, three weeks at the other. So David and Mike suggested taking Ron and his bike to Mike's auto repair shop where they would try to make an emergency repair. Ron was skeptical, but after considering the available options, he accepted the offer.

David and Mike considered various repair schemes. One of them suggested putting a pin through the spindle, but after discussing the matter further, they agreed that the alloy probably wouldn't hold a pin. Next they talked of removing a cottered steel crankset from a junked bike that they had seen at a local salvage yard and installing it on Ron's Motobecane. But Ron remarked that a mechanic at one of the shops had told him that Motobecane used Swiss threading on those cups. That made cup switching impossible; so whatever changes might work, they were stuck with using the original cups.

Could they adapt the Selecta spindle to a surplus steel cottered crank? That seemed unlikely, but it got them thinking about ways to use the splined spindle. Mike wondered whether pieces of steel welding rod could be installed to replace the worn off crankarm ridges. If so, they could force fit the crank back onto the original spindle. However, they would have to shape the hole in the crank to accept the rods to make the plan work.

"File it out?" Ron asked.

"File teeth would fill up too fast," Mike said.

At the shop, Mike laid a piece of bare ⅛-inch welding rod over a groove in the spindle to check the fit. It looked promising. However, they had to devise a way to cut grooves in the crank to accept the rods. The steel washer embedded in the outer end of the crank bolt hole was in the way.

"That washer has to go," Mike said.

He clamped the crank vertically in his vise. Then with a

hacksaw he made a vertical cut from the upper end of the crank to a point just below the washer. He located this cut just far enough from the outside surface of the crank to reach the washer. After making the vertical cut, he turned his saw and made a horizontal cut across the crank below the washer. When this cut reached the vertical slot, the slab of alloy fell off the crank and exposed the washer. Mike picked off the washer, leaving a hole through the crank as large as the spindle—actually a bit larger because of the damage, as shown in the bottom figure in illustration 2–1.

Now to find the appropriate tool for making new grooves in the crank. Mike shuffled his tools, picked up a tungsten carbide rod saw blade, and fed it through the hole in the crank. He removed the blade from the hacksaw he had been using and attached the rod saw. Then he began to saw a groove where there had been a ridge. (Remember, the welding rod pieces had to replace the ridges in the crankarm, to mate with the valleys in the spindle.) The rod saw worked beautifully. It was small enough to make the grooves needed, and yet it didn't fill with the soft alloy waste material as he worked.

After sawing out the eight grooves, Mike got a piece of ⅛-inch welding rod and broke off the flux coating. Then he cut pieces of rod just long enough to reach from the inner surface of the crank to the inner side of the washer when it was replaced. He tested the grooves he had made by holding a piece of rod up to each. A perfect fit isn't necessary for this kind of installation. The alloy will permit a drive-on fit if the grooves are close to the right diameter.

Mike drove the small rods into the fresh grooves, starting with those grooves around the lower section of the crank hole. Then he inverted the crank in the vise and drove in the remaining pieces. The rods were driven into the crank from the inside surface of the crank toward the outside. To hold them in place, Mike used a tapered punch, again driven from the inside surface. The tapered punch forced the rods firmly into the grooves. With Mike's practiced eye this was a quick job; a neophyte would probably have to make frequent comparisons with the spindle.

The next step was to drive the crank onto the spindle, as shown in illustration 2–1. Mike held a short steel cylinder against the crank and hit the cylinder with a ball peen hammer while

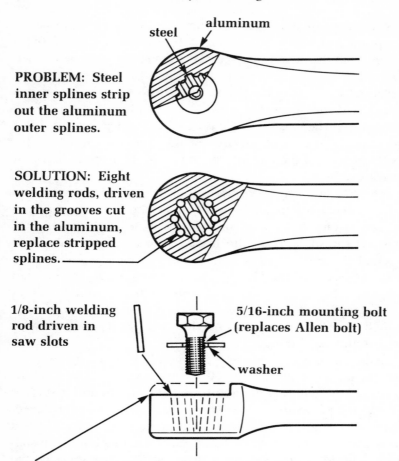

PROBLEM: Steel inner splines strip out the aluminum outer splines.

SOLUTION: Eight welding rods, driven in the grooves cut in the aluminum, replace stripped splines.

steel   aluminum

1/8-inch welding rod driven in saw slots

5/16-inch mounting bolt (replaces Allen bolt)

washer

Remove metal to washer (1/4 inch) to expose splines for cutting and insertion of welding rods. This cross section shows the modifications necessary to reattach the arm to the spindle.

Illustration 2–1. Detail of quick fix of damaged crank.

the opposite crank was supported by a wood block. The cylinder he chose was about 1½ inches in diameter, large enough to cover the rods in the crank.

The washer and bolt were replaced and made snug. Then each of the men tested the bike.

Ron: "It goes."

Dave: "You can stand on the pedals. No slack."

Mike: "With more surface making contact, it may be better than new."

They tried the bike out on a steep hill about a mile from Mike's shop. Then Ron gathered his gear and rode off into the sunset, yelling, "perfect." Of course, one can only speculate how long this kind of repair might last.

We pass this story along to make a couple of points. One is that when you embark on a bicycle tour, you should be prepared for every eventuality. Ron was fortunate to run into a pair of resourceful mechanics. The main point of the story can be expressed in the old addage, "an ounce of prevention is worth a pound of cure." If only Ron had carried along the appropriate tool and taken the trouble to tighten his cotterless cranks before leaving, he would never have needed this custom repair.

We hope you will profit from Ron's mistake. Carry the tools you need to maintain your touring bike in good working order. Check the parts most prone to loosening often enough to prevent disaster. But if the worst happens and you strip a splined crankset or develop some similar problem, try to convince a bike mechanic that it can be repaired, or find an all-purpose fix-it shop similar to the one Mike runs. You could do worse—such as being forced to choose between a long layover for parts or shipping your bike home.

Part Three
Planning Your Tour

Touring—Alone or in a Group?

Bicycle touring in any fashion—solo or group—can be a wonderful and broadening experience. However, as with any vacation or trip, you need to do some careful planning before jumping on your bike and riding off into the sunset.

How to Choose a Group Tour

If you are new to touring, an organized group tour may be a good way for you to break in. Of course, cycling with a group has its disadvantages along with its advantages. When you travel in a group, you must be willing to make some sacrifices and compromises. At the same time, however, you have other people with whom to share the day's experiences and make plans for the upcoming day.

Traveling with a reputable touring organization not only offers you the camaraderie of a group, it also provides you with experienced leaders who can anticipate potential problems and help alleviate them. That can be very comforting, especially if you are not already an experienced cycle-tourist. But, before signing up for an organized tour, explore all the available options. Find out about the reputation of the organization by talking to people who have traveled with it before. Make certain the trip you choose is the right one for you! If you're not quite sure what questions to ask, the following should give you a place to start.

When considering a particular tour, ask yourself, "Does this place really appeal to me?" Sure, it may look terrific in the brochure. But, before you spend the money, find out as much as you can about the location. What will the terrain be like? How do you get to your starting location? And will you end at this point or somewhere else? What kind of physical condition must you be in to endure—better yet, enjoy—this particular type of tour? Also, consider the climate and time of year. If you want to see spring blossoms or fall foliage, ask when the weather conditions would be most suitable.

Tour Members

What about the people you will be spending all this time with? Are they singles, couples, natives of the area, or foreigners? What is their average age? Having a variety of personalities certainly makes for a more educational and stimulating adventure. At the same time, if you are in your late teens and all the other people signed up for the tour are in their mid-forties, you may feel a little out of place.

How many people will be in the group? Do you prefer traveling in a large group or a small one? And how many of these people will be tour leaders? What are their qualifications? What experience do they have in conducting group tours? Have they had any of the formal instruction that is now offered through various cycling organizations? If you are traveling to a foreign country, are they able to understand or speak the language or will a translator be provided?

Support

Will a support vehicle accompany the group? These vehicles, otherwise known as "sag wagons," offer definite advantages, as they are usually equipped to handle gear, luggage, spare parts, maybe even your souvenirs, allowing you the freedom from carrying a heavy load. They've also been known to carry a few exhausted cyclists.

Ask how much baggage you can take. With a large group it may be limited. Will one driver be assigned for the duration or are group members expected to take turns at the wheel? If so, are adequate maps and route information provided?

If the tour is to be a camping trip, must you provide your

Photograph 3–1. Before signing up for an organized trip, find out who the leader or leaders will be and what kind of qualifications they have for the job.

own equipment or can this be rented from the organization?
Do you have the option of bike rentals in foreign countries or
must you transport your bicycle as well as yourself to your
starting point?

Food and Shelter

Ask what type of lodging will be provided. Will it be hotels,
country inns, hostels, camping, or a combination of these? Make
sure these arrangements are suitable to you. Ask the organization
for a brochure depicting the accommodations in detail.

How will meals be served? Will you be expected to provide
certain meals on your own? If camping, does everyone pitch in
with the cooking and clean-up duties? Is there a menu planned
in advance, and where does the food come from? Depending
on your location, will sufficient information be provided ena-
bling you to explore some of the local cuisine? Food and housing
are very important, so don't hesitate to ask a lot of questions
about them.

Other Details

Ask for specifics about each day of the tour. How far will
you ride in one day? How heavily traveled is the route? What
kind of sightseeing can you expect, and how much time will be
allotted for it? Are these extra activities part of or in addition
to the tour price? Oftentimes you are not obliged to stay with
the group and can spend some time touring at your own pace.
If you opt to travel off by yourself, are detailed maps and iti-
neraries provided?

Another item to consider is accident insurance. If this option is not offered, you may want to look more closely at your
policies for coverage.

Are adequate rest stops built into the itinerary? Naturally,
as the tour lengthens, more rest stops should be taken into
consideration.

No brochure, no matter how lavish or extensive, can anticipate and answer all your questions. So read between the
lines of fine print, shop around, and ask plenty of questions.
Find the tour that will best suit your needs, your lifestyle, and
your wallet.

The Joys of Solitary Travel

If you are independent by nature and blessed with a spirit of adventure, you may prefer to travel alone instead of with an organized group. This was true of Terry Fletcher, a young woman from San Francisco, who at the age of 21 and over her family's objections, decided to tour Europe alone. Terry felt that no organized tour would take her to all the places she wanted to visit. She preferred to retain her freedom to pick and change routes as she wished. Also, she felt it would be senseless to travel all the way to Europe only to spend all her time with a group of Americans.

What Terry discovered on her five-month tour is that traveling alone makes you feel vulnerable, so you tend to reach out and make friends quickly with people whom you meet along the way. In middle June, when she began her journey, the roads of Europe were crowded with bicycle tourists. In Holland, she saw entire families—from grandparents to small children—touring by bike. When she got lonely, she found it easy to find other tourists going her way for a few days.

Ironically, Terry's short-term travel companions included a tour group of American college students, but she also traveled for a time with a young Dutch woman who was, like her, embarked on a solo journey. Other companions along the way were three 16-year-old German boys with whom she could barely communicate and two New Zealanders on their way from Denmark to Yugoslavia.

Terry found that campsites and youth hostels are excellent places to meet other young people from all over the world. Also, friendships were made through chance encounters on the streets of a city, out on the open road, in parks, or on beaches. One day in September, Terry took shelter under an awning during a thunderstorm in a little town near Florence. After a while, a young Italian girl ran across the street to speak to her in broken English. The girl ran back home to get her English textbook, then returned and shyly asked Terry to help her with her homework. In this way, another friendship developed.

There are obvious drawbacks to traveling alone in an unfamiliar place. Though Terry says she generally felt safer while

around Europe than she does walking on the streets
n hometown, she did have a few unpleasant experi-
certain countries, she was propositioned quite a bit,
possibly because the men of those areas assumed that only a
"wild and crazy" American girl would travel alone by bicycle.

Despite the drawbacks, Terry strongly feels that she would
not have met as many different people nor experienced the
various European cultures as fully as she did had she traveled
with others for the entire trip. Her best souvenirs are the addresses of numerous friends with whom she now corresponds
in such faraway places as Buenos Aires, Gdansk, and Cairo.

But whether you choose to go it alone or in an organized
group, Terry Fletcher is one tourist who is convinced that the
only way to experience the fullness of countryside, mountains,
and forests of places like Europe is to travel by bicycle. Young
Americans whom she met who were traveling by Eurail seemed
to be on a wild race to cover as much territory as possible
before their passes ran out. They had apparently seen nearly
every train station in Europe but not much more. Traveling by
bicycle, you are not only able to have more intimate experiences
of the land than those who choose other modes of transportation, you also have a much better chance of experiencing the
friendship and hospitality of the people who inhabit the territory
you are visiting.

Touring Information

If you plan to go on an organized cycle tour, you will need
to contact the appropriate organizations. To make this task easier, *Bicycling* magazine annually compiles and publishes a list
of more than 100 group touring organizations. Included in the
list are names, addresses, phone numbers, and tour locations.
Information in this listing has been approved by the tour groups
and does not constitute an endorsement by the magazine. For
a copy of the latest list, send $1 to Organized Group Tours,
Bicycling, 33 E. Minor St., Emmaus, PA 18049.

Those of you interested in planning your own tours may
find it helpful to look at the brief descriptions of tour routes
submitted by readers of *Bicycling* and published as a regular

feature in the magazine. More detailed information on each set of these tours, including maps, can be obtained by request from the magazine. Just follow the instructions provided at the end of each tour article.

Touring in the Winter: A Firsthand Report

What's the first thing you do after deciding you want to attempt touring in the winter? After determining whether you're crazy or not, you seek out the most reliable advice you can find. What we have come up with is the following firsthand report from avid racer and cycle-tourist, Robert Templin.

Preparations for a Journey

Canada to Mexico on bicycles—it doesn't seem like such an outrageous proposition when you first think about it, except that we were going to do it in three weeks in the middle of winter. Eighteen hundred miles and some of the worst weather that the Pacific coast had experienced in over a decade separated me and my riding companion, Al Woolum, from Tijuana, our goal.

The first stop in preparation for our Super-Tour was a camping equipment supplier, Adventure 16 in San Diego. People there recommended rain gear made of Gore-Tex, a fabric both waterproof and breathable, a combination unheard of a few years ago and ideal during the wet and cold months of the winter season. Gore-Tex fabric has been improved since it first hit the market, so make sure you buy equipment using the latest version; it's much more efficient, and it's easier to take care of than its predecessors.

The outfitter also explained how to dress for touring in cold weather often intensified by the wind. One set of warm bulky clothes is not nearly so versatile, he pointed out, as several thin layers of clothing, which you can peel off or put on as the weather changes. We were glad we took his advice and bought wool, as it still retains some warmth after getting wet. The machine-washable variety, if available, is best.

The layers we chose for our cold Pacific coast ride included the following: long underwear (top and bottom), wool tights, long-sleeve wool jersey, wool knee-high socks (the kind used in cross-country skiing), and a windbreaker. Two layers of wool on the legs (the knees especially) are advisable for protection. When it was really cold or raining, we would wear the Gore-Tex pants and jacket. A wool ski mask was also a must.

For our hands, we had glove liners (Space Age Glove Liners by Aris) under wool gloves, plus overmitts with waterproof palms. Unfortunately the tops of these let water in, which feels miserable hour after wet hour. Next time we'd wear Gore Tex overmitts instead. We pedaled in wool socks, regular cycling shoes (with a spare set of Bata touring shoes) and Cinelli shoe covers, which didn't keep our feet dry in the rain. Waterproof covers would have been better. For us the only solution to cold hands and feet through Washington and Oregon was to make as many café stops en route as possible for hot chocolate!

The second source we drew from was a good bike shop—for names of other cyclists who had done this kind of touring before. We also wanted advice on the most reliable touring equipment since mistakes one can get away with in the summer may prove quite dangerous in the middle of a winter storm. As it turned out, the Kirtland bags we chose performed admirably under the conditions we encountered. For extra protection we plastic-bagged anything we didn't want to get wet. Of course, in the rain, fenders are a must. Lightweight, plastic models are best; they don't rust, and bend easily when required. Get some mud flaps for the fenders unless you and your riding companions like the taste of tire-flavored water.

About three or four months before the trip, I wrote the various public agencies that disperse free information on the areas that we'd be traveling to. Caltrans was especially helpful in California, giving us special maps for bicycle riders coming down the coast. Write state transportation departments for free maps and other useful road information and chambers of commerce, tourist bureaus, and other public agencies for free information on specific locales.

Touring in winter requires some unique adaptations on the

Photograph 3–2. When touring in winter, it is wise to allow for some time to be lost because of bad weather. But if you must ride in rain or snow, be sure to wear clothing that will keep you dry.

part of the cyclist. When planning, remember there is less riding time than during the summer. We usually had to stop for a campsite by at least four every afternoon if we wanted to eat dinner and get everything set up by dark. And by all means, allow at least one or two days of little or no riding each week. This will give you a cushion for days when you take side trips or encounter really bad weather. We, unfortunately, had to keep to a tight schedule, and this necessitated riding 14 of the 21 days we were on the road in medium to heavy rains.

Several shakedown cruises to test out equipment are recommended, and anyone undertaking a major tour in the winter ought to be in fairly good physical condition, prepared to ride on flooded, icy, or nonexistent roads. Know the symptoms, consequences, prevention, and treatment of hypothermia—and if you do start to feel weak, dizzy, or as though you can't get warm, take shelter. Mental toughness helps on days when the rain seems endless or when the 50-mph wind is blowing right in your face. (If you're not as stubborn as Al and I were, you can hitchhike or stay in hotels when the going really gets rough.)

Cold weather can play havoc with knees and other parts of the body, so take it easy the first few days and get adjusted to the conditions. As for the bike, keeping it reasonably clean and lubricated is important because when you're pedaling wet roads, you're washing off the chain lubrication. For some help against flats, use tire-savers with fenders since they brush off debris your hands can't reach.

If you do all this, what do you have to look forward to? You'll enjoy riding roads deserted by tourists and recreational vehicle traffic and thus get a better view along the way. Plus, it's quite a special feeling to do battle with the elements and win.

A Few Select Memories

Survival. Any biologist will tell you that in order for a species to survive in an ever-changing environment, it must adapt to those particular changes. "Big Al" (his stocky, six-foot-five-inch frame more than justifies the title) and I were trying our best to adapt, as the violent rain pelted the deserted Washington coast road we were attempting to pedal down. I say "attempting" because the road more resembled a river than a route for two- and four-wheeled travel. "Where's our paddles?" Big Al wanted to know. So did I.

It was the start of a new year, January 1, and the beginning of our adventurous tour from Canada to Mexico. "Thank goodness for football," Al commented as we made our way through Port Angeles in northern Washington. He was referring to the traffic-free roads, thanks to all the football games slated for television that day. The open road and lush Northwest forests made the cold rain more bearable as we passed isolated towns that appeared lifeless except for the smoke rising from the over-worked fireplaces. Al and I considered ourselves experienced cyclists, but our journey back home to Southern California would be a lesson in humility, as well as a revival of our faith in the "human experience"—people reaching out to help one another in difficult times.

The response we received at a small café in Sappho, Washington, was typical of the welcome we would experience the length of the tour. Our mode of travel in the ever-present rain drew more than a few stares as we leaned our bikes against the wall. But as we peeled off our Gore-Tex rain gear, it became obvious to the onlookers that we hadn't acquired our dark tans from "these parts." We were definitely outsiders.

"Where you from? Where you headed to?" the waitress asked in rapid-fire succession. It wasn't long before Al and I were being offered rides, a place to stay, and even a family dinner. We politely turned down the offers for a ride, explaining that our tour was a fund-raiser for the Lung Association, and we received pledges for every mile traveled. As for the family dinner, well, that was another matter. Anything had to be better than the beans and franks fare to which we had become accustomed.

The retired Oregon couple will probably long remember the pair of cyclists that came to their home to eat—and eat. I'm sure they planned on having ham leftovers for at least a week, but Big Al (his appetite applies here as well) and I devoured the spread like the hungry cyclists we were. Our hosts informed us that they hadn't seen such a performance since their own children left years ago.

Our trip was basically a tour—full camping gear—but these occasional stopovers with the local "coast people" (as Al affectionately referred to them) provided us with more than just a colorful insight into the region we were traveling through. It gave us a chance to learn more about ourselves through the eyes of others and an opportunity to appreciate what others have to offer in the ultimate lesson: coping with and adjusting to the differences among human beings. After all, here we were, a couple of city boys, encountering firsthand the lifestyles and attitudes of a slower-paced rural world. It gave another meaning to the word "survival."

Like any typical tour, ours included an appreciation of the physical beauty of the land as well as an enjoyment of the people met along the way. Though Al and I battled wet, icy roads; muddy pot-holed paths; and sometimes, nonexistent highways (we traveled Highway 1/101 most of the 1,400 miles), we wouldn't hesitate to make the trip again. We had picked an especially foul winter for our tour; the headlines along the route continually shouted from the newsstand: "Storm Lashes Coast," "Worst Weather in a Decade," and "Northern California Braces for New Storm."

So why would we do it again? Besides the inherent adventure value, we saw the coast in a completely different light than the summer cyclist usually does. Little or no tourist traffic to clutter the road, rugged coastline made all the more awesome with each new, brutal front that passed through, and a chance to challenge a new environment—all are important reasons for considering a return engagement.

Several days before we reached the Mexican border, the warming sun made a rare appearance, which lifted our spirits. We had adjusted to wet weather the past three weeks but didn't mind making the transition back to warmer (and drier) days— after all, it "never rains in Southern California." I lost track of how many rain songs we learned (like "Raindrops Keep Falling on My Head" and other favorites). As we made our way through Long Beach, California, Al looked over at me and stated half-seriously, "I think we just might make it." Just then a tractor-trailer rushed by and almost blew both of us off the road. It was time to start readjusting to the long-forgotten mores of the Southern California roadways and methods of surviving them.

Photograph 3–3. Al Woolum and Robert Templin riding along the Pacific coast on their way from Canada to Mexico.

Outsmarting the Desert Sun

This summer, when thousands of touring cyclists hit the road, many of them will be pedaling across arid or semiarid territory. This is particularly true of southern, transcontinental cyclists like those leaving Los Angeles and heading east. If desert riding is in your plans but you're not quite sure what to expect or how to prepare, here is the advice of David J. Wisniewski, a cyclist who has spent many summers touring in Arizona and Nevada.

Planning

The best place to begin your desert riding is at home with some accurate, detailed maps in front of you. When dealing with the desert, you must realize that towns, for example, don't always exist where the map says they do. Therefore, good maps are important. I suggest writing to the tourism or transportation departments of the states in question and requesting state-supplied road maps. They seem to yield the most useful, accurate information in relation to map size. Of course, these won't provide the detail that topographic maps will, but you won't have to spend a wad of money on state-issued maps or devote a third of your luggage space to them, either.

Don't try using pages cut from a road atlas. I once learned that the hard way; where I eagerly anticipated a town, I found just two turned-over trailers and a rusted-out car—no meal, no water, no town.

While perusing your maps, be very deliberate in choosing your route since you don't want to wander around aimlessly in 100° heat. If your purpose is solely to cross the desert and be rid of it, pick the most direct major highway available—an interstate highway if one is handy. Out in the desert, you get very few hassles from law enforcement people about this. Besides, you stand a better chance of getting by with less problems or getting help if you need it on a road like this.

If your emphasis is more on scenery or your timetable is more relaxed, go ahead and ride the lesser roads, but be certain you have the route figured out in advance and try to stick to it. Don't take any spur-of-the-moment side trips without careful consideration—the desert is not forgiving of error.

Making It through the Days

The extreme heat on a desert crossing will determine how you pace your daily rides. Probably the most practiced approach is to rise early, in the predawn hours if possible, and start riding with the first light. This enables you to travel during the coolest part of the day—which, by the way, doesn't last very long. Many people think they can ride comfortably until about noon, but the only real comfort you'll feel is in the presunrise hours. A typical low-desert summer day, like those in the California and Arizona low-altitude deserts and along the Colorado River valley, begins with a predawn temperature no cooler than 75°; usually it's higher. After the sun appears, you can expect a jump of about 10° the first hour and 2° to 3° per hour after that until the temperature begins to peak around one o'clock. And forget the stories about the desert turning really cold at night. Usually this occurs only if you have a couple of thousand feet of mountain below you.

Cyclists with average tolerance to heat can ride efficiently until about 11 o'clock in the morning. By then it pays to have pinpointed a town where you can spend the afternoon. I suggest sitting out the inferno near a source of water, particularly if your body is not very heat-efficient. You'd be surprised how much water you can gulp down in an afternoon, even though you're just waiting around. That's why it's not smart to roadside it out on the open desert for a whole afternoon when you're carrying a limited supply of water.

Just when to resume riding is open to speculation. Many tourists hit the road again around four o'clock, thinking that the worst of the heat has passed. In actuality, peak desert temperatures extend from about one to five in the afternoon, with a very slow decline thereafter. It doesn't begin to "cool off" effectively until after the sun has dipped below the horizon. This will become dramatically clear the first time you experience a desert sunset. It feels as if someone has suddenly pulled you out from under a heat lamp.

So I suggest waiting to depart until about an hour before sunset, then pedaling off what you can in the remaining hours before total darkness. In this manner, you can still do a good eight hours worth of riding for the day. To repeat, I caution against trying to put in a continuous day of normal pedaling while in the desert.

Maintaining adequate food and water supplies while in the desert is of critical importance since the availability of these two precious items is often limited or, in some cases, nonexistent for many miles. Be prepared to devote a good deal of cargo space to water. I've found that during my most efficient periods of desert riding I still require a pint of water for every ten miles ridden in order to feel normal.

Carrying the amount of water needed to get you through a stretch of about 100 miles can create some problems. It's best to split the load as much as you can. Putting water in one-pint

Photograph 3–4. When riding in the desert, take along plenty of food and water and don't try to put in a complete day of pedaling.

plastic bottles, the kind normally sold containing fruit juices, will help balance your load and assist you in pacing your water consumption. Carrying all your water in one bulky container not only makes for bike-handling problems, but it also places your entire water supply at your fingertips whenever you opt for a drink. This can get you into trouble because once you start, it's often hard to stop.

When the sun really beats down on you, it's very tempting to douse yourself with water but don't unless you definitely have enough water set aside to last you to your next source. Normally, I prefer to see the water going into my stomach, where it will ultimately do more good in combating the heat.

What should you wear? Along with your shorts, it's best to wear a loose-fitting shirt or something with a mesh front to admit a free flow of air. Breathable wool jerseys are also a good choice. Stay away from 100 percent nylon jerseys, though, or you'll be a veritable rolling greenhouse.

One thing you have going for you here is the dryness of the desert air. If you can arrange it so that you get a flow of air through to your upper body, you'll be in pretty good shape. Try to do this short of removing your shirt or jersey. It's a mistake to go unprotected under the desert sun for a prolonged period of time, even if most of your riding is during the morning hours.

Likewise, be sure to protect your head with a helmet or at least a cap. One of my favorite tricks on extremely hot days is to wear an old cap and carry a little extra water so that I can keep the hat fairly wet; when the head is kept cool, the body responds a little better. Unless you already possess a golden tan, be sure to protect the exposed areas of your body with sunscreen lotion. Painful burns develop very rapidly out here, particularly if you're fair skinned to begin with.

Spending the Night

Camping will be uncomfortable, especially if you can't manage to end each day at a reasonable altitude. As I said previously, the desert floor remains quite hot all night. Sometimes sleep is an impossibility. I recall riding through a 115° day on tour—

125 miles in about ten blistering hours. My reward that evening was an overnight low of 94°, coupled with a 20-mph wind that made the inside of my tent feel like Dante's Inferno.

If you are bound and determined to camp, try to stay in a legitimate campground. Camping on the open desert leaves you vulnerable to running out of water overnight or having your camping area invaded by a rogue's gallery of unwanted pests, not the least of which are snakes. If campgrounds are not available and you must make do with the open sand, try to find a stand of bushes or scrub to pitch camp by. This makes a slightly cooler camping area.

If you can plan your days to end at higher altitudes—on mountain or mesa—do so and then stick to the plan. Your chances of attaining some comfort are increased. Also, if you are lucky enough to have a picnic table at your site, think about bedding down on top of it. It will probably be more comfortable than anything you can rig up on the hot ground.

On long rides in the desert, I usually go the motel route. Normally, I'm a diehard camper but not here. I look for a shower and a soft bed. It means sacrificing some mileage sometimes or adding on some to make sure I reach a town, but it's worth it!

Part Four
Preparing and Maintaining the Touring Body

Speed Training for Tourists

Bicycling is a speed sport—not just for racers but for serious touring riders as well. Consider these two cycling scenarios, both true.

Scenario One. August, 1981. Bear Mountain, New York. The nine-man lead breakaway of the Senior men's national road championship swept through the last miles of their 105-mile race. A road sprint was certain. The smart money, from knowing observers, went to either Larry Shields of California or Jeff Bradley of Iowa, both savvy road racers with explosive sprints.

Suddenly, a quarter mile from the finish, Tom Broznowski, a virtual unknown from Seattle, burst to the front. Shields jumped on his wheel and passed him less than a hundred meters from the finish. It seemed a perfectly timed move, and Shields must have been smiling in satisfaction.

Then, in a shocking come-back, Broznowski launched a second explosion. He upped his cadence to an even higher level, sprinted past Shields, and regained the lead 20 meters from the line. Even before he'd crossed the line, Broznowski's arms were spread in a gesture of triumph. Just behind, Shield's face wore an unbelieving expression of despair. He'd been taught a hard lesson in road sprinting.

After the race, Broznowski told his secret: "I attribute my road sprint to my track racing experience. Without track riding, I don't think I could have made the moves that won this race for me."

In a later interview, he elaborated further. "Track racing

works for me. It provides my interval and speed work. Looking back at the nationals, even if Larry Shields hadn't jumped by me, I probably could have led the sprint out and won it that way. It was just like sprinting at the track. These road riders don't practice their sprints enough. Without practice, how can you expect to do it when the time comes?" Broznowski's point, and you can bet it wasn't lost on his competitors, was that if you want to develop your acceleration and speed, you need to practice exactly that.

Scenario Two. One hundred fifty miles into the Seattle-to-Portland double century, a lone rider waited patiently at a traffic light. He'd been riding alone, against a stiff headwind for over two hours. Even though he'd prepared diligently for the ride, his long lone effort into the hostile winds had unexpectedly sapped his strength.

Then, something happened that made him forever change his view on training for touring rides. Just as the light turned green, a well-formed paceline of six riders swept by on his left. Joining their paceline, he knew, could spell the difference between finishing the final upwind miles in good form or struggling along in a "death march" mode. He quickly tightened his toe straps and sprinted away from the light. But by the time he'd reached cruising speed, the six riders were 300 meters ahead.

Their speed closely matched his, but try as he might, he couldn't close the gap. The prospect of finding shelter in their paceline tantalized him to increase his cadence, but fatigue and lack of speed training prevented him from jumping quickly across the gap. Finally, after 7 or 8 miles of Herculean effort, he joined up. However, the damage had been done. His 8-mile solo time trial had depleted his last reserves. At the first hill, he lost contact and finished the last 40 miles alone and shattered.

During that final 40 miles, our unfortunate rider must have cursed his inability to sprint across the gap. It's a move he'd seen racers perform time and time again, but he'd never dreamed he'd want to use it on a touring ride. Now he knew better.

"Speed development training is relevant for both racers and serious recreational riders," says Mike Kolin, former coach of Rebecca Twigg and coauthor of *The Custom Bicycle* (Emmaus, Pa.: Rodale Press, 1979), *The Ten-Speed Bicycle* (Emmaus, Pa.: Rodale Press, 1979), and *Cycling for Sport* (Seattle: Velo Sport

Press, 1984). "It's easy to sell racers on the concept, but touring riders are skeptical. Nevertheless, there are dozens of everyday cycling situations that are made easier by developing your speed potential."

Speed Isn't Just for Racers

A faster jump and a higher top speed will benefit touring and commuting riders in several ways. For one thing, these skills will make riding in traffic easier and safer. In fact, any cycling situation in which you must accelerate frequently from a dead stop will be made easier by developing your jump. Lane changes, merges, left turns, and other such maneuvers can be executed quicker and more safely.

An increase in your speed will also enable you to more easily close those gaps that inevitably form on any group ride. Even the most laid-back touring groups can become separated at traffic lights, on hills, and by traffic. If you can quickly close the gap to the leaders, the remainder of your ride will be more enjoyable and physically easier. You can't always expect the leaders to stop and wait. Sometimes you have to chase. "When you have to close a gap in a paceline, don't cruise up; it's physically less demanding to snap across the gap," says Kolin.

Building up your top-speed potential and acceleration is an integral part of any well-rounded training program. Everyone agrees that long-distance endurance, hill-climbing ability, and bike handling are important for all riders. Speed training is no different.

Assessing Your Potential

As you are probably aware, there are different kinds of human muscle fibers. The two with which we are most familiar are the white or "fast-twitch" fibers and the red or "slow-twitch" fibers. Slow-twitch fibers don't react as quickly as fast-twitch, but they have great endurance. Fast-twitch fibers, on the other hand, contract very quickly in extremely short bursts of explosive energy. They are generally stronger than slow-twitch fibers, but they tire more quickly.

Each of us has a certain ratio of fast-twitch to slow-twitch fibers in our muscle system. The higher your percentage of fast-twitch fibers, the greater potential speed you have. A biopsy is needed to determine the precise percentage, but this is unnecessary for our purposes. You can learn through experience how much "natural speed" you have. What we want to do is suggest a training program that will help you more fully develop the speed with which you are naturally endowed.

Developing Your Training Program

An axiom of most sports training programs is that the only avenue to superior ability in a particular activity is to focus most of your attention on it. This means that if you want to build up your speed, you have to do a lot of fast riding. There are no special tricks or short-cuts available, you simply have to push top speed over and over again. This is how Tom Broznowski won the Nationals. As coach Mike Kolin observes, "he'd ridden that same sprint a couple dozen times already that season during his velodrome training."

Mike Kolin and most other coaches prescribe interval training as the core of any speed-development program. Intervals are short bursts of exercise at near-maximum effort. Their goal is to force your heart rate up to the point where your body is operating near its maximum oxygen uptake level (VO_2 max). The length and pace of your interval effort depends on the event for which you are training, your level of experience, and of course, your level of commitment.

In fairness, your commitment level should vary according to your reasons for undertaking the training program. If your only goal is to improve your speed for touring and recreational riding, there is no point in subjecting yourself to the kind of painful training regimen that a racer must adopt to be successful.

A typical interval program for a prospective racer would begin with the riding of a short distance—say a half mile—at a pace roughly 10 percent faster than he would be able to maintain

Photograph 4–1. One of the most popular forms of training for speed is interval riding—periods of maximum effort interspersed with more relaxed pedaling for partial recovery.

over a continuous, ten-mile course. After completing that distance, he would pedal comfortably for a couple of minutes to allow his heart rate to drop to about 120. This process would be repeated as many times as possible, until ten intervals could be ridden at the chosen pace. At that point, the pace would be increased another 10 percent, and the whole process would be started over. Speed workouts of this type are very tiring and should not be done two days in a row nor more than three times a week.

Alternatives to Interval Training

The most widely adaptable alternative to interval training is *fartlek,* a Swedish term meaning "speed play." The principle behind fartlek is to alternate speeds during the course of a run or ride but in a playful rather than a rigidly controlled sort of way. Psychologically, this is easier to do than perform a series of intervals. As you are out on a recreational ride, you may decide to sprint up a hill or toward a road sign that appears up ahead. A car may pass you, and you decide to chase it for a while. The possibilities are limited only by your resolve and imagination.

The weakness of fartlek workouts is that because the location and duration of the fast segments of your ride are left undetermined in advance, you may be tempted to not push yourself very hard. One way to lessen this possibility is to ride with a group of friends since peer pressure will help keep you from sloughing off. You may also find that you will have to make some sort of mental commitment in advance to ride hard during certain segments of a familiar course.

Group rides offer other possibilities for speed work. Members of the groups can take turns attacking, with the rest of the pack hanging back until a sizable gap opens, then bolting across the opening in pursuit of the leader. And, of course, if you really want to subject yourself to group pressure, try entering a few local road races. Races themselves can be used as valuable training sessions.

Photograph 4–2. Training with friends can be a useful and enjoyable way to do speed work. Each member of the group can take a turn jumping away from the pack and opening a gap before the others bolt forward in pursuit.

Some forms of speed work can even be practiced on easy riding days. Try floating up a hill, then spinning instead of free-wheeling all the way down the other side. Keep your cadence high and concentrate on smooth pedaling. The physical demands are slight, but through this high-rpm riding, you improve your form and train your legs for hard speed work.

Sprinting Technique

There's more to going fast than developing your fast-twitch muscles. Superior sprinters have also developed superior technique. The ability to go fast involves more than spinning the pedals quickly; you must also be able to spin a high gear very quickly. Most riders can pedal a 70-inch gear at 150 rpm, but only a few world-class sprinters can keep that same cadence while pushing a 97-inch gear. (See page 16 for an explanation of how gear inches are determined.) How's it done?

First, carefully build up your fitness through long winter and spring aerobic road miles. Start in low gears—63 inches is a common early season choice—and gradually work into the 70s and 80s. If you're working to develop your pedal speed, as all sprinters must, stay in the low gears until you can comfortably spin at a cadence of over 100 rpm for a long training ride. Once you've upped your gearing into the 70-inch range, in the spring and summer, add the interval or fartlek training just described. With the proper fitness base, you'll avoid any injuries that may come from pedaling big gears too soon.

During your interval workouts, practice proper arm technique. Maximum acceleration is impossible without using your arms. When the right foot is pushing down on the forward part of the pedal stroke, pull up on your right arm. At the same time, you naturally use your left arm to keep your bike tracking in a straight line. The process is reversed during the left foot's power stroke. Always sprint with your hands on the drops. You need the combination of an aerodynamic riding position and hand placement that gives good leverage.

During your interval or fartlek workouts, strive for a smooth 360-degree power circle. Physiologically, it's impossible to apply power evenly, all the way around, but some riders come much closer than others. Make every effort to pull up on the pedals and then smoothly shift to a pushing motion at the top of your pedal stroke. Are your buttocks bouncing on the saddle during a hard sprint? If so, your pedaling stroke is too rough. Backtrack into lower gears and devote more practice time to high-cadence pedaling.

In an all-out sprint, slide forward to the tip of your saddle. This arches your back, which adds force to your power stroke. It also helps your arms pull on the handlebars, and since your elbows are bent, you'll be more stable if you get bumped from the side by other riders.

As a touring cyclist, you may never need the kind of speed and strength employed by Tom Broznowski to double-jump his way to a nationals victory. You may never even enter a road race of any kind. Nonetheless, by practicing some of the techniques described in this chapter, you will find yourself becoming a faster, stronger, more confident rider, and that can be a valuable asset in helping you have a safe and enjoyable bicycle tour.

Food for Touring

Touring cyclists are especially conscious that they use food for fuel. Anyone who has "run out of carbs" 50 miles from nowhere can testify to the miseries of trying to go on without putting some more fuel in the tank. Many cyclists are unconscious, however, of what is the best type of fuel for their bodies. As a form of exercise, touring demands high energy output for extended periods of time. Whereas most recreational marathon runners can knock off 26 miles in three to four hours, a day's touring may last six to eight hours or even longer. Even though they're usually not racing, touring cyclists are moving under a load that may require equivalent amounts of energy expenditure.

Many tourists make the mistake of eating lots of sweet and sugary things to give them "energy." This type of food may be helpful in sprints because the simple sugar is rapidly absorbed into the bloodstream and is quickly usable as an energy source. For endurance exercise such as touring, however, it is inappropriate. A large sugar load in the bloodstream causes the pancreas to secrete a large amount of insulin to deal with the sugar. The sugar is then rapidly used up by the body to meet its increased energy demands. Insulin, on the other hand, causes the body to store excess sugar rapidly. This combination of rapid use and rapid storage will leave endurance athletes with a temporarily low blood sugar level, which is experienced as fatigue, headache, and nausea and in some extreme cases may lead to loss of consciousness.

When touring, what you need is an energy source that isn't metabolized (burned up) so rapidly. A good, well-balanced diet from a wide variety of whole foods is the way to satisfy these energy needs. You should try to derive 65 to 70 percent of your total calories from carbohydrate sources. However, most of these calories ought to be obtained from complex carbohydrates such as potatoes, vegetables, whole grains, and legumes (like beans or peas). Complex carbohydrates take longer to break down into forms useful as fuel than do the simple carbohydrates found in candy, pastry, fruit, and juices. Thus, hypoglycemic symptoms caused by rapid increases in blood sugar are avoided. Also, their slower rate of metabolism means the complex carbohydrates can provide fuel steadily over long periods of time.

Fat should be limited to 20 percent or less of your total calories, and try to get most of your fat from low-fat dairy products such as yogurt and cheese made from low-fat milk. Use vegetable oils that are high in essential fatty acids, such as safflower and sunflower oils, for salads and baking, and use lower fat nuts like sunflower seeds and walnuts for munching.

Protein should also be limited to 20 percent or less of your total calories. Studies have shown that even body builders require no more than 1 to 2 percent more protein than the recommended daily allowance (RDA), which is about 9 percent of total calories. This is plenty of protein to repair the muscle tissue that breaks down while riding.

Get Off to a Good Start

It's best to start the day with a good breakfast about 1½ to 2 hours before departure (to allow your stomach time to empty). Cereal with low-fat milk, or whole grain pancakes with a little butter and syrup or honey, are great. Keeping your stomach fairly empty will keep you comfortable while riding. To do that, you will have to eat a small amount of food several times during the course of a day. It follows, then, that you should avoid large meals in the middle of the day. They tend to make you uncomfortable, and it is difficult for your body to provide ample blood supplies for digestive purposes when much of your circulation is moving to your legs during exercise like bicycling. A heavy meal preceding heavy exercise may cause stomach upset and certainly will slow you down.

Try carrying raw vegetables—like carrots, celery, bell peppers, and cauliflower—in your handlebar bag to munch on while you ride. An apple or other fruit is fine once or twice a day, but watch out for high sugar loads; the fructose in fruits is a simple sugar. Granola is a good snack food, but remember that many granolas are very high in fat, so read your labels, or better yet, make your own to control the fat content. A loaf of whole grain bread is light to carry and a good source of energy. If you feel compelled to put peanut butter on it, go very light—peanut butter is loaded with fat—or if you like to munch on nuts, keep the same warning in mind. Remember to keep the calories derived from fat under 20 percent of your total.

Your evening meal can be more substantial than the others and can be the time you load up some good carbohydrates for use on the next day of riding. A good choice of food in this case is pasta, preferably whole grain, which is more nutritious than processed (white) types. Pasta is lightweight, requires only hot water to fix, and is high in complex carbohydrates. If you want a variation from tomato sauce, try grating on some low-fat mozzarella or Parmesan cheese, or top the pasta with butter and a mix of herbs.

Don't worry about consuming a little higher percentage of fat in your evening meal; you'll probably need it as part of your total calorie intake. After all, touring cyclists may need as much as double the normal person's calories to maintain their weight. This may mean consuming 3,500 to 5,000 calories per day.

Be adventurous in trying new foods and combinations of foods. Even simple road meals can be gourmet in taste while being lightweight, nutritious, and adequate to meet the energy needs of an endurance athlete. By carrying salad dressings and a small container of herbs such as basil, dill, oregano, cumin, and thyme for flavorings, you can make the simple foods you cook very tasty. One special food worth including in your list is garlic. It is lightweight, tasty, and has been shown to be anti-inflammatory. Garlic is also an immune stimulant and a help in lowering cholesterol and triglycerides, while elevating HDL, the type of cholesterol that has been shown to be protective against heart disease. It also opens up the blood vessels and breathing passages to increase oxygen to the tissues (muscles).

Drink Up, Drink Often

Water is extremely important to the cyclist, whether it's hot outside or not. Water losses often go unnoticed because the air passing over your body as you cycle tends to evaporate perspiration, so it may not seem as if you're sweating as much as you really are. During the course of a day on your bike, your body will lose a lot of fluids, which must be replaced if you are to prevent dehydration. You can't go wrong with water. A small amount of lemon squeezed into your water will give it some flavor and limit buildup of mucus in your mouth. Diluted fruit juices are another option, as are electrolyte replacement drinks, although some should be diluted more than their labels indicate. On hot or very windy days, you may need to drink a gallon or more of fluid over the course of a day's ride. Also, when cycling at high altitudes, you need to drink a lot. According to Ed Burke, Ph.D., dehydration is the main cause of symptoms associated with altitude discomfort. In less severe circumstances, you can drink less.

Don't wait until you are thirsty to drink. If you do, you may already be in too great a fluid deficit, and there may not be any

Photograph 4–3. These brownies, the seafood pasta, and the oatmeal are high in complex carbohydrates, vitamins, and minerals. The frozen Fruit and Cream will melt into a high-vitamin and -mineral snack.

water around. Sip a little fluid frequently, every 15 minutes or so, and keep your water bottles as full as possible so you never run out completely.

Follow these dietary guidelines during your bicycle tours, and your energy needs should be adequately met. However, because of the extra stress that you are placing on your body, you may wish to add a good multivitamin as a supplement to your touring diet.

Sample Recipes

We conclude this discussion by presenting a few recipes that have been developed with the needs of touring cyclists specifically in mind. Try them out, if they appeal to your tastes, and create your own specialties as well.

Peanut Butter Brownies

These brownies are packed with complex carbohydrates for sustained energy, but go easy on them since they are also high in fat. We recommend using a natural peanut butter that contains no added oils or sweeteners. If only a few brownies are taken for the trip, the rest may be frozen and eaten on another escapade. **Developed by Ann Sheridan.**

¾   cup peanut butter
¼   cup oil
½   cup honey
½   teaspoon vanilla extract
2   eggs
½   teaspoon baking powder
⅓   cup whole wheat flour
½   cup quick-cooking rolled oats
½   cup chopped walnuts
½   cup raisins

In a small mixing bowl, combine peanut butter, oil, honey, vanilla, eggs, and baking powder with electric mixer or by hand until smooth. Stir in flour and rolled oats until completely mixed in. Stir in walnuts and raisins. Spread into oiled 8 × 8-inch pan. Bake in 350°F. oven until lightly browned, about 25 to 30 minutes. Cool completely before cutting.

Yield: 16 brownies

Fruit and Cream

This snack is excellent to take along on day trips. Prepare the evening before; freeze overnight; and place, still frozen, into your pack. After several hours, the ingredients will thaw into a high-carbohydrate, high-vitamin and high-mineral snack that is light and creamy. **Developed by Susan Burwell.**

1   cup fresh or frozen strawberries (thawed if frozen),
        pureed
1   cup chopped fresh or frozen peaches
½   cup chopped fresh or frozen cherries

1   cup vanilla ice cream
1   cup cooked brown rice
⅛   teaspoon nutmeg
1–2 tablespoons honey (optional)
3   tablespoons toasted coconut

In medium-size bowl, stir together strawberries, peaches, cherries, and ½ cup ice cream. Set aside. In a small bowl, combine remaining ice cream, rice, nutmeg, and honey if desired. Divide fruit mixture in half. Spread one half into the bottom of four empty yogurt cups or one-cup containers. Divide rice mixture into four equal parts. Spoon rice evenly on top of fruit. Spread remaining fruit evenly on top of the rice. Top each cup with coconut. Cover and freeze.

Yield: 4 servings

Sea Shells

This recipe is ideal for the athlete involved in long, strenuous activities. Not only high in carbohydrates, this dish also replenishes the electrolyte minerals—such as magnesium, potassium, calcium, and phosphorus—that may be depleted during several long days of touring. (Note that oysters and clams are higher in these minerals than tuna.) Carry seasonings and cheese and a small container of butter or oil on the bike, then stop to buy the remaining ingredients at a grocery store. **Developed by Susan Burwell.**

8   ounces small shells or other small pasta (3 cups dried
      pasta)
¼   cup olive oil or butter
2   7-ounce cans minced clams, oysters, or flaked tuna,
      drained
1   tablespoon dried parsley or 2 tablespoons minced fresh
      parsley
1   clove garlic, minced, or ½ teaspoon garlic powder
1   teaspoon Vegit or Mrs. Dash herb seasoning
     black pepper to taste
1   cup plain yogurt
2   tablespoons grated Parmesan cheese

Cook shells in boiling water until al dente. In large skillet, combine oil or butter, seafood, parsley, garlic, herb seasoning, and pepper. Heat until mixture bubbles. Remove from heat and stir in yogurt and cheese. Drain cooked pasta and toss with seafood mixture.

Yield: 3–4 servings

Oatmeal on the Road

The dry ingredients for this recipe can be mixed together quickly at home. Dehydrated apples can be found in the raisin section of the supermarket or in health food stores. Buy apple juice on the road—those paper boxes of apple juice are perfect for this dish. **Developed by Ann Sheridan.**

1   cup quick-cooking rolled oats
1   teaspoon cinnamon
⅔   cup instant nonfat dry milk
⅓   cup roasted sunflower seeds
2   tablespoons chopped dried apple pieces
2   cups apple juice

Mix rolled oats, cinnamon, dry milk, sunflower seeds, and apples and seal in a plastic bag. At breakfast time, boil apple juice. Shake the dry oat mixture, then stir it into the juice until well blended. Cover and let sit a few minutes before serving.

Yield: 2 servings

First Aid Kits for Tourists

Dr. Clifford Graves is a retired surgeon and a renowned cyclist. He escaped the Germans at the Battle of the Bulge on a bicycle; he has traveled all over the United States and a good part of the civilized and not-so-civilized world on a chromed folding bicycle built by the legendary Rene Herse. Yet, despite all the miles he travels, he refuses to carry a first aid kit of any kind. His reasons for this are three-fold:

- Minor problems don't need any treatment.
- Major problems can't be taken care of by a first aid kit.
- You aren't going to have what you need, anyway (Murphy's law).

Still, we would be willing to bet that the always-prepared Dr. Graves would know just what to do in any roadside emergency and would somehow conjure up any needed medical supply out of his little handlebar bag.

We think there is something to be said for carrying a first aid kit along when you set out on a bicycle tour. True, the most important first aid item to take with you will not be found in any kit. It is the knowledge of what to do in an emergency. If you know that, you will know what else to take with you. If you don't know what to do, carrying medicines and bandages will be useless—even harmful if you misuse them. But if you have good general knowledge about how to treat injuries, then some sort of kit can come in handy.

Prepackaged Kits

There are two ways to go with first aid kits: prepackaged and do-it-yourself. If you prefer the convenience of a prepackaged kit, there are several types from which to choose. Most readily available is the basic first aid kit sold in most corner drugstores. It contains only a few items such as Band-Aids and first aid cream.

More elaborate kits can be purchased through mail-order outfitters. These are basically of two types: outdoors kits, which contain items that are useful for hikers or mountain climbers but unnecessary for most cyclists, and survival kits meant primarily for people lost in the wilderness. The outdoors kits may be useful to off-road cyclists riding wilderness trails, though they are quite expensive and include some items that may be hard to replace.

Finally, there are small, compact kits put together especially for cyclists, which contain an assortment of gauze pads, plastic strips, antiseptic swabs, and the like for treating not-too-serious road rash, minor lacerations, and similar afflictions to which cyclists are prone.

Outdoors Kits

On the whole, an outdoors kit seems to be the most complete approach for those who don't want to try to assemble their own. The kit should be in a waterproof container, should not be too big to carry by bike, and should contain common-sense items for cyclists rather than exotic supplies for mountain climbing emergencies. Let's examine two of these kits to see what's in them.

The first kit is sold by Early Winters and is known as their Type II kit. It is the smaller of their two kits. It comes in a multicompartmented bag small enough to put in a large handlebar bag, but it is not fully waterproof—five minutes in a direct water shower wet the contents closest to the zipper. The nylon shell material is coated with a waterproofing substance, and the contents should be adequately protected in all but the most torrential downpours when carried in a good quality handlebar bag or pannier. For extra protection, you can place the whole thing in a plastic bag or put the contents in small plastic bags inside the kit. The Type II kit contains the following, with our comments added in parentheses:

- 1 bandage scissors
- 1 splinter tweezers
- 1 razor blade (for shaving hairy spots before taping)
- 6 safety pins
- Betadine antiseptic skin cleanser (soap and water is just as good but not as neatly packaged)
- 2 plastic pill boxes (supply your own pills to go in them)
- 1 small vial (holds the razor blade, safety pins, and two dimes)

- 1 triangular bandage
- 2 18 × 36-inch gauze bandages (for bleeding wounds)
- 2 2-inch × 5-yard gauze bandages (for holding the above in place, etc.)
- 1 roll Dermicel tape (to secure dressings)
- 5 2 × 8-inch muslin strips
- 10 4 × 4-inch gauze pads
- 10 plastic strips
- 1 small first aid dressing (compress), Carlisle model (a very hefty pressure dressing, straight from the army surplus store)
- 1 pair vinyl gloves in plastic bag
- 2 wire tags
- 4 accident report forms (for mountaineers; goes into detail about helicopter evacuations)
- 1 pencil
- 2 10-foot strips fluorescent marker tape (to guide helicopter)
- 1 emergency/survival handbook (fairly complete; center pages are silvered to us as signal mirror)

The suggested retail price in 1984 was $49.95.

The Early Winters Emergency Medical Kit I is about twice as large as the Type II. We think most cyclists would find it too big to carry except in a pannier bag, and like the Type II, it does not have a fully waterproof container. It contains some extra supplies such as more bandages. It also contains the following, not found in the Type II:

- hypothermia thermometer (reads 75 to 105°F.)
- 1 4 × 30-inch wire splint (for immobilizing fractures; a good idea)
- poly squeeze bottle (supply your own liquid medicine to go in it)

The suggested retail price in 1984 was $64.95.

Early Winters also sells the following items separately: *Mountaineering First Aid* book, *Hip Pocket Emergency Handbook,* hypothermia thermometer, bandage scissors, gauze compress, wire splint, and Sting-Eze to relieve insect bite itch and pain.

Cyclist's Kits

First aid kits sold especially for cyclists are smaller, easier to carry, but sacrifice the elaborate completeness of the larger outdoors kits. The important thing is that their smaller size makes it practical to carry one at all times. We looked at sample kits from three companies: Bailen, Alpine Aid, and Alpine Map Company.

The Bailen kit is the smallest. It comes in a $3\frac{1}{2} \times 4 \times 1$-inch plastic box, contoured to fit a cycling jersey or hip pocket. Its box will provide limited water protection, but it leaked enough to wet the contents when subjected to our five-minute direct shower. It has room only for the following:

- 3 Telfa (nonstick) pads
- 6 plastic strips
- 1 foil packet of antibiotic ointment
- 2 foil packets of antiseptic ointment
- 1 foil packet of A & D ointment
- 1 foil packet of petroleum jelly
- 2 alcohol swabs
- 6 aspirin tablets

The suggested retail price in 1984 was $5.65.

The Bikit from Alpine Aid (makers of Kangaroo Baggs) contains mostly basic first aid supplies, with a few extras, in a zippered nylon bag. The fabric is waterproof coated, but its zippers and seams are not waterproof. The contents became soggy after five minutes under a shower. Included in the Bikit are the following items:

- 1 roll of $\frac{1}{2}$-inch adhesive tape
- 6 3 × 3-inch gauze pads
- 12 plastic strips
- 4 Telfa (nonstick) pads
- 1 matchbook sewing kit
- 1 single-edge razor blade
- 8 aspirin tablets
- 2 small books of nonwaterproof matches

- 2 butterfly closures (for repairing small lacerations instead of suturing)
- 4 safety pins
- 1 bar of soap
- 4 knuckle bandages
- 1 first aid book

The suggested retail price in 1984 was $15.95.

The Madden Cyclist Emergency Kit from the Alpine Map Company is the only one here that is truly waterproof. The eight-ounce, 5½-inch-long tube didn't leak a bit when subjected to the shower or submerged. This kit contains the same first aid supplies as the Alpine Map Pak-Kit survival kit discussed below, but leaves out some of the bulkier and less necessary items such as the signal mirror, whistle, energy bars, bouillon cubes, and tea bags. On the whole, it is a good kit for those who want to carry some survival items, but not a whole pound of them. The suggested retail price for the Cyclist Emergency Kit in 1984 was $12.95.

Survival Kits

It is hardly practical to carry additional medical supplies, even (or especially) if you are going to be out in the "boonies" for extended periods of time. It's probably more important to carry sufficient food and supplies to allow being stranded in the wilderness for several days. The Alpine Map Company addresses this need with their Pak-Kit, which contains the following supplies:

- 8-foot tube tent
- signal mirror
- high-pitch whistle
- basic first aid supplies
- emergency instructions
- candle, 2 flaresticks
- 50 waterproof matches (will still light after being immersed in water)
- 20-foot nylon cord

- aluminum foil
- 3-foot duct tape
- dextrose cubes, "energy bars"
- 3 bouillon cubes
- waterproof container
- Celestial Seasonings herbal tea bags

This kit weighs one pound and is pretty big—8 inches long by 2¾ inches in diameter. The tubular case, capped at each end, is waterproof. The suggested retail price in 1984 was approximately $15.

Most prepackaged kits contain some sort of antiseptic, such as Johnson and Johnson First-Aid Cream or Betadine. However, the best wound cleaner is usually soap and water. Scrapes and cuts should be thoroughly cleansed; if there is any ground-in dirt, it should be removed by scrubbing if necessary. (Cyclists are tough and can stand pain.) Cyclists should carry some soap, either bar or liquid, and a water bottle that has not been drilled out. As an alternative, there are now appearing on the market disposable scrub brushes containing soap and water. These are primarily designed for surgeons, but you may be able to obtain them at a surgical supply house. A similar product, FREPP Wound Cleansing Scrubbers, made by Marion Scientific Products, may also be available and is very handy.

Keeping the Kit "Up"

A medical kit will not do you much good if it has been depleted of supplies. Whether a purchased kit or do-it-yourself kit, the best way to keep it up-to-date is to include a list of contents in the kit. Whoever uses the kit is responsible for comparing the list with the contents and replacing anything that is missing. Also, it's a good idea to check kits containing medications every three months and replace any that are about to go out-of-date. Sterile supplies that have gotten wet should be replaced, as they will no longer be sterile. Before going out on a bike ride, check that you have your kit with you, just as you might check your tires and water bottle.

Conclusions

If you decide to prepare your own first aid kit, then you must use your own judgment and creativity in making it as complete as possible without turning it into an unwieldy burden for your bike. But if you are inclined to purchase one of the prepackaged kits, then we have some final general observations to make about them.

For those of you who want a very complete kit, we would say that the Early Winters Medical Kit II would be a logical choice. It's biggest drawback is its price—$49.95. But if you want something smaller and less expensive, then one of the cyclist's kits might be your best choice. The Bikit and the Bailen First Aid kit contain little that cannot be obtained at your corner drugstore. However, if you try to put together a kit of this type, you will have to pay the price for the prepackaged quantities offered on the drugstore shelves. These kits are convenient and contain what you need to treat minor cuts and scrapes.

Credits

The information in this book is drawn from these and other articles from *Bicycling* magazine.

"How to Shop for a Touring Bike" John Kukoda, "Sport Touring: Pleasant Surprises in the Market" and "Loaded Touring: Ready for the Long Haul," *Bicycling,* January/February 1985, pp. 48–63.

"Transforming Your Present Bike into a Touring Machine" Darryl Skrabak, "The Touring Machine," *Bicycling,* April 1982, pp. 60–64.

"Racks and Panniers: Where to Put the Weight on Your Bike" Darryl Skrabak, "Fore or Aft? High or Low?" *Bicycling,* April 1982, pp. 78–82.

"The ABCs of Training for Touring" Susan Weaver, "The ABCs of Training for Touring," *Bicycling,* April 1983, pp. 35–37.

"Traveling Light" Robert Templin, "Going Light," *Bicycling,* April 1982, pp. 72–73.

"Seven Tips to Make Your Touring Easier" Harvey T. Lyon, "Plastic! And Six Other Tips to Make Your Touring Easier," *Bicycling,* April 1982, p. 58.

"An Ingenious Repair Can Save Your Tour" David Weems and Mike Murphy, "The Repair That Can Save Your Tour," *Bicycling,* June 1984, pp. 144–46.

"Touring—Alone or in a Group?" Delores Nash, "Group Touring . . . How to Choose the Best One for You," *Bicycling,* April 1984, pp. 86–87; Terry Fletcher, "The Joys of Solitary Touring," *Bicycling,* April 1983, pp. 81–85.

"Touring in the Winter: A Firsthand Report" Robert Templin, "Firsthand Report: What You Can Expect From Touring in the Winter," *Bicycling,* September/October 1982, pp. 60–62.

"Outsmarting the Desert Sun" David J. Wisniewski, "Outsmarting the Desert Sun," *Bicycling,* May 1982, pp. 21–23.

"Speed Training for Tourists" Barclay Kruse, "Speedwork and Play," *Bicycling,* August 1984, pp. 44–47, 153–57.

"Food for Touring" Konrad Kail, "Food for Touring," *Bicycling,* July 1984, pp. 60–63.

"First Aid Kits for Tourists" David L. Smith, "First Aid Kits," *Bicycling,* May 1984, pp. 44–49.

Photos and Illustrations

Frank Berto: photo 1–5; T. L. Gettings: photo 3–2; Mark Lenny: photos 1–2 and 1–3; Patti Seip: photo 2–1; Robert Templin: photo 3–3; Christie C. Tito: photos 4–1 and 4–2; Sally Shenk Ullman: photos 1–1, 1–4, 1–6, 2–2, 2–3, 3–1, and 4–3; Bonnie Wong: photo 3–4. George Retseck: all illustrations.